POSTCARD
THE BEACH

POSTCARDS FROM THE BEACH

PHIL TUFNELL
WITH PETER HAYTER

CollinsWillow
An Imprint of HarperCollinsPublishers

First published in 1998
by CollinsWillow
an imprint of HarperCollinsPublishers
London

© Phil Tufnell 1998

1 3 5 7 9 8 6 4 2

A CIP catalogue record for this book is
available from the British Library

ISBN 0 00 218842 2

Photographs supplied by Winston Bynorth

Printed in Great Britain by
Caledonian International Book Manufacturing Ltd, Glasgow

Contents

Acknowledgements

My thanks to Lisa and Poppy for putting up with me being away, and for putting up with me being home again; and to my colleagues on the 1998 England tour to the Caribbean for their thoughts and input and for giving me something to write home about; to our scorer Malcolm Ashton for his kind permission to reproduce items first published in *The Thrutcher*, to Darrell Hair for giving out a left-handed batsman offering no stroke to me bowling over the wicket and, finally, to my co-author Peter Hayter for all his hard work and that £60 glass of port.

Phil Tufnell

To Mary, Max and Sophie, thanks once again for your support; to Tom Whiting and Chris Stone for their industry, to my associates in the press corps for their assistance, and to the players for their help in recalling parts of this hectic tour the memory of Phil Tufnell could not reach. To Winston 'Muttley' Bynorth, half-man/half-dog/half-photographer. And to the cat for his enthusiasm and frankness and for not spilling a drop of that £60 glass of port, thanks ol' boy, and can I have my tape recorder back now, please?

Peter Hayter

Introduction

What you are about to read is all true, as far as I know. My intentions in compiling this diary of the 1998 tour to the West Indies were two-fold. First, to place on record the events on and off the field that go to make up the extraordinary business of life on an England cricket tour. Second to make a few bob. Please buy and copy of this book, preferably two. Every little helps.

P.C.R.T

CHAPTER ONE

Shut up and make the will

Friday 2 January, Copthorne Hotel, Gatwick

Me, Philip Tufnell. England's controversial left-arm spinner. Off on another tour to the Caribbean. With my reputation?

For the seventh time in eight winters since I first knock-kneed onto a British Airways Jumbo bound for sunny climes, I arrive at the point of departure to meet up with the rest of the chaps.

My wife Lisa and baby daughter Poppy have been kissed, cuddled, waved goodbye to and placed in the pending tray. For the next three months or so my family will be fifteen other cricketers, plus tour manager, coach, assistant coach, physio, fitness coach, press officer and scorer all similarly disconnected from home, loved ones and 'normal' life in pursuit of the little red ball. I took Poppy into the garage at home while I packed up my cricket 'coffin'. There she was sitting in her pushchair, looking a bit bemused. Was I imagining it or did she look a bit sad?

Jollied up by the usual preliminaries, including a tale from Graham Thorpe, henceforth 'Chalks', whose first experience after being put in charge of our dress code indicates he is quite clearly not cut out for the job . We have all been issued with regulation casual wear. All right, actually; smart blazers and strides, etc. The trousers being worn by our pugnacious left-hand batting genius, however, seem, strangely, a shade darker than the rest. And why is that?, you may ask.

As it turns out he took them to the dry-cleaners last week in order to have them taken up to fit his tiny little legs and when he went back yesterday to pick them up, the shop was closed. Standing there lobbing stones at the upstairs window to try and attract attention, he did; the attention of the local constabulary. The officer in question accepted his clearly ludicrous explanation but a request to break the door down was denied. Hence his current state of mis-dress .

What may be in store came into clear view yesterday when I went to make a will. The bloke takes one look at me and says: 'You're doing this because you think Courtney Walsh and Curtly Ambrose are going to kill you, right?'

I say: 'Shut up and make the will.'

FOCUS. That is the word from now on. We focus on last-minute words of encouragement from Supermac, Lord MacLaurin of Knebworth, Chairman of the England and Wales Cricket Board, our ultimate boss. 'Good luck, Athers,' he says to the skipper. Good luck, Angus,' he says to Gus Fraser, 'take plenty of wickets.' 'Ah, Tufnell … you will *try* not to get into any trouble, won't you?'

He must have the wrong bloke.

Saturday 3 January, London Gatwick to Antigua

Here we go again. Aeroplanes.

Cabin crew crosscheck, doors to automatic and prepare for take-off … The words I fear more than any others in the English language. St Christopher in my mouth, clutching the armrests so hard that the blood drains from my fingers. Bumpy start brings back memories of scariest ever flight:

November 1990, first tour, Australia; from Adelaide to Port Pirie to play against a South Australia Country XI. Strapped into a little wah-wah rolling and lurching through an apocalyptic storm, like being trapped in a tumble drier. Either nutting the ceiling or trying to keep the contents of my stomach inside my stomach. Halfway through the flight the stewardess reassuringly burst into tears. Laurie Brown, our physio, began handing out the medicinal Famous Grouse shortly after take-off. The bottle didn't last the flight.

This time, worst fears not realised. Eight hour flight passes without incident and, thanks to the prescribed three or four Scotches, without pain. Leave England in the pouring rain. Arrive in Antigua in brilliant sunshine. God is in his heaven.

Sweep through customs and on to Jolly Harbour, our home for a week of pre-tour acclimatisation. On site is the new super-duper Caribbean Cricket Centre which we are due to inaugurate in a match against a celebrity side including Mali Richards, son of the Masterblaster Viv, before moving on to Jamaica. At the moment, however, playing surface is underwater due to three days of storms. Give up and hack down to the beach for some giggly slip catching. Many balls lost at sea.

Venture down to the bar to discover that the resort is all-inclusive, as in THE DRINKS ARE FREE. Me. Philip Tufnell. At an all-inclusive resort where the drinks are free. With my reputation?

Sunday 4 January, Jolly Harbour
Wake up Philip, we're here.

Wrist and shoulder niggling me. Left wrist hurt while bashing the boxing gloves in pre-tour training at Old

Trafford. Not great. Shoulder also aching slightly and I may have to have a cortisone injection. What is more, it is raining hard so our already slim prospects of practice are wiped out immediately. Not much better at home. Ring Lisa to find out that Poppy is ill.

Siesta, then karaoke night in the bar. Lots of Americans whooping loudly and Germans peering at them disgustedly. Mark Butcher is pushed forward to represent us. Much chortling from those who don't know he is a professional standard guitar player and singer and he slays them with a faultless, note-perfect rendition of Marvin Gaye's *I Heard it Through the Grapevine*. I give them *My Way* which I thought was appropriate but return to the group to be greeted with lots of nervous coughing.

Monday 5 January

Rain and gales. Before last week they hadn't seen a drop here for seven months. We turn up and it hoses down. This has happened so often before on England tours all over the world that the thought occurs that every drought-stricken nation should arrange a Test series against England. Within days their reservoirs would be filled to overflowing.

Inevitably the facilities are again unusable. But if any of the boys had been hoping for a couple of quiet days away from the ruthless fitness co-ordinator Dean Riddle, (who, me?) another think very soon arrives. 'Bumble', otherwise known as David Lloyd, our wildly enthusiastic-about-everything coach, has found a place for us to practice fielding.

The resort's helicopter pad is flat, but the drawback is that from time to time helicopters actually do land on it, causing us to hit the deck like extras in *A Bridge Too Far* to avoid being decapitated by the rotor blades.

Afternoon at leisure, as they say. I try out water-skiing and jet skis. Invent a new method of water-skiing that involves being dragged along belly first. As I ride out on the jet ski I fail to notice the dirty big black clouds making their way towards me. Too late, I turn and try to outrun them back to the beach. When the rain comes it drives at you hard as buckshot and obscures the shore. All this leisure is tiring me out.

Return to witness the efforts of our keenest fishermen, Robert Croft and John 'Creeps' Crawley. All the villas back on to the marina here. The boys drop their lines over the balcony into the water and wait. Creeps strikes early and hauls in the most grotesque looking fish I have ever seen. It has the teeth of a beaver. Croft goes to pull out the hook but stops himself saying: 'I'm not putting my hand in there.' The fish starts to writhe and thrash about, so Bumble sticks his foot on it. There follows general consternation as we attempt to figure out how to finish it off. No-one has a clue. Finally Croft, the Welshmen's Jack Hargreaves, emerges from the kitchen with a blunt cutlery knife and proceeds to saw its head off. Possibly not the textbook 'kill', but it was the fish or us.

Tuesday 6 January

The appearance of the twice-weekly Antiguan newspaper *The Outlet* starts us thinking about what is in store. Under the back page headline 'ENGLAND ARE HERE' is a photograph of a group of us at Gatwick airport. But more significant is an article by Michael Holding, the great West Indies fast bowler known as 'Whispering Death', on their captaincy controversy.

By now it has emerged that Brian Lara had been the first choice of the West Indies selectors to lead them in Pakistan, but that their decision was blocked by the Board, who insisted on retaining Courtney Walsh instead. Following their 3–0 defeat against Wasim & co, there are strong moves for Walsh to be sacked in Lara's favour. All kinds of factors will be taken into account including what Lara calls his 'indiscretions' and the fact that the first Test takes place in Jamaica, Walsh's home island. Also, there have been suggestions that if Lara replaces Walsh, the fast bowler will quit playing altogether.

The West Indies Board are due to announce their decision on Thursday, here at the Cricket Centre, where, coincidentally, Lara and Walsh will be attending a players' association meeting. Holding writes: 'Were there any suitable candidate other than Lara, I would advocate that a new man must be appointed now. On the field I have no argument with Lara – he is clearly a better captain than Walsh. But he has followed his own agenda beyond the boundary and that could set the wrong example. The Board should turn to him only if he is prepared to devote 100% of his attention to the team by cutting out some of his other interests.'

Oo-er, missus., to quote the late great Frankie Howard. Nice to have people worrying about someone else's captain for a change.

Try to have a net but it chucks it down again, so the spinners get together for a chat about what we are here to do and how we are going to go about doing it. Bumble, Athers and Jack Russell join Emburey, Croft and myself to discuss what we will try to do to their batsmen … and what they will try to do to us.

For Lara I'll be looking to bowl wide of the off stump with four fielders on the off side to try and restrict him. We discuss me bowling over the wicket to Carl Hooper if there is enough rough outside the leg stump to bowl into, because he considers such tactics insulting and just tries to slap every ball. My general thoughts about the approach of West Indies batsmen to spin bowlers are that the very sight of us brings out the macho man in them and they immediately try to knock us out of the game. This can be a failing. Will *those* words come back to haunt me?

Athers and Bumble impress upon us the need not to panic if the bombs start going off. Easier said than done.

The batsmen also had a meeting and each of the specialists has adopted a tail-ender as a batting 'buddy'. It's the job of the buddy to keep an eye on what the senior player is doing in the nets, to supply the throw-downs to help him get in the groove, etc. And it is the job of each of the senior batsmen to try and help squeeze a few more runs out of their tail-ender. Mark Ramparakash, my 'buddy', has clearly drawn the short straw.

One aspect that Bumble and Athers are keen to emphasise is how vital it is to keep the scoreboard ticking over with singles. A batsman can get so caught up in trying to survive the barrage that he can play an outstanding defensive innings, technically faultless, survive for an hour and a half in bomb alley, then look up at the board and realise that the sum total of all his efforts, blood, sweat, tears etc, is 4 not out. We must avoid that at all costs.

While taking a late night libation in one of the bars, we spot Lara in a dark corner. I go over and he stretches out a hand to shake mine. Lara in his lair.

Wednesday 7 January

All the rain gags have been exhausted. But the sight of the island of Montserrat on the horizon is a reminder of what can happen here if nature really gets the hump. When the wind is blowing in the right (or wrong) direction, the volcanic ash still blows right across the ocean here to Antigua. For a while the restaurants in this resort had to serve food in takeaway containers to prevent it being covered in a thin layer of soot.

Four years ago we stayed far from here at Dickenson's Bay in the Halcyon Cove Hotel. One of its attractions was the fact that if you fell sideways out of the rooms you would land in a bar called Miller's on the Beach, the scene of some post-Test Carib and rum and coke celebrations. When Hurricane Louis hit the island the following year, causing massive damage, Miller's was completely flattened. Those who took a trip there this time without prior knowledge came back reporting a hole where it used to be.

I check the instruction sheet on what to do in the event of a hurricane, viz.:

WHAT TO DO WHEN THE HURRICANE WARNING IS GIVEN' (Tempted to write in 'Run like f***').
Do not pay attention to rumour.
Put away all objects which can be blown away by wind such as furniture, flowerpots etc., since they can be destructive weapons during the hurricane. (HEADLINE: In an incident insiders are describing as 'bizarre' England's controversial left-arm spinner, Phil Tufnell was last night struck and killed by a flying Spirea Japonina).
Avoid taking alcoholic drinks. Not sure about that one.

DURING THE HURRICANE
Open one of the windows or doors of your house on the side opposite to the one from which the wind is blowing. Remember to close the same door or window as soon as the direction of the wind changes and open another contrary to

the new direction. This is recommended as a means of balancing the pressure inside and outside the house, so that the difference in pressure does not tear away the doors or windows.

(Now I know why they recommend that you avoid taking alcoholic drinks. One thought: what if the piece of paper, on which all this is written, blows away? See 'Run like f***'.)

Rain has washed out any chance of nets for the fourth day in a row. The only bowling I've done has been on the road outside the villa. Difficult to find the competitive edge when you are bowling at a bottle of Evian water on a strip of concrete. Croft is worried that he is not turning it. Er, we're bowling on a road, Robert. Beam us up, Scotty.

We must get out of here and find somewhere dry to play. There is no way we can play this match on Sunday so why don't we say sorry and cheerio?

To Galley Bay for lunch with co-author, plus Mark Butcher, Nasser Hussain and Mark Ramprakash. On the way, discover whole new (Caribbean) meaning to the expression 'if that'. Prior to leaving we ask a bloke at reception how long it will take to get to the restaurant. 'Ten minutes' drive,' he says, 'if that.' Three-quarters of an hour into a journey on one of Antigua's finest not-quite-finished roads that is making me carsick, we realise the full implications of the words 'if that'. More like 'Ten minutes' drive, if that. If not that, an hour and a half.'

By the time we arrive I am green and prepare for the meal by orally evacuating into a flower bed. The food is grim and the whole experience crowned when for the first time anywhere, ever, I am sledged by a waiter. After informing us of today's dessert specials he announces: 'Very good to see you Englishmen here at our restaurant and I thank you for coming to visit us. Mr Tufnell, you goin' home in a body bag.'

Thanks.

On our return, we discover that we are indeed escaping tomorrow morning. Although everyone here has been very helpful and tried everything possible, the boredom induced by inactivity means that we are getting out not a moment too soon.

Things looking a bit strange at the moment. There are already rumours that the newly-laid pitches in Jamaica and Trinidad might not be great, that the political problems in Georgetown, Guyana following the elections, i.e. bombs and a grenade at the Pegasus Hotel where we are due to stay, has put that Test at risk and that the rebuilding at St John's, Antigua means that ground and another newly-laid pitch might not be ready in time for the final Test when we come back at the end of March. Sorry, when was this tour arranged?

Thursday 8 January. Antigua to Jamaica

The news we have been expecting arrives. Lara has been given *the* job. Mixed reactions among the boys. Inevitable, I suppose, after West Indies have just lost 3–0 in Pakistan under Walsh. We all know Brian and what he is capable of. What concerns me more is that, captain or not, he's still going to be out there with a bloody bat in his hand. Lara's supporters insist that the captaincy will make him more 'responsible'. (Funny how they never thought of that in my case.) Bit of speculation over whether Courtney will now take his ball and go home, especially as, historically, hardly any former West Indies captains have played on under their successor – Viv Richards and Richie Richardson certainly didn't. I doubt if Walsh will jack it in. He tells reporters: 'I'll have to decide if it's something I can live with', but Courtney is a top bloke and he wants the 25 wickets that would take him past Malcolm Marshall's record for the highest number by a West Indian, badly. Still, he seems to be playing hard to get, and some behind the scenes negotiations might be in order.

We devise a cunning plan. Jack Russell is a good mate of his from their years together at Gloucestershire. Jack is briefed to take the big man out to dinner and wind him up, along the lines of 'Ere, Courtney, you're not going to take that, are you? Be a man. Walk tall, make a stand, bugger off.' Jack is not convinced.

Meanwhile we arrive at the airport early morning to find that there is a balls-up with the flight. Oh really? The two main carriers here are LIAT. and BWIA, which stand for Leeward Islands Air Transport and British West Indian Airways, or something like. Unkind observers have other names, like Leave Island Any Time and Luggage In Another Terminal, and for BWIA, Believe it When In Air.

Usual delays, so pass the time nattering and looking around the duty free. Come across an advert extolling the virtues of Bill Abbott, 'the Samson of the West Indies'. Big photo of a bloke who must be seventy if he is a day, holding in his stomach and flexing his saggy pecs. Laden down with more jewellery than Liz Taylor, he sports a black syrup that looks like someone spread marmite on his head. Above pictures of him with Robert Mitchum, circa 1950, are lists of his accomplishments, as follows: Cricketer, Wrestler, Strongman, Swimmer, Diver and Street combatant, and Footballer, Boxer, Dancer, Table Tennis, Entertainer and Fakir. Could he be the all-rounder for whom England have been searching for so long?

After waiting for an hour or so to get on the plane we are

stuck on the ground for another while they go off in search of a passenger who has apparently left his bag on a seat and unilaterally disembarked. When he eventually returns, someone asks him where he's been. He looks at the man with utter contempt in his eyes and squeezes one word out of the side of his mouth. Lunch.

Get earache on the plane from some woman plugged into the inflight music channel belting out all the songs at the top of her voice. Then, from time to time, and for no apparent reason, she picks up her metal walking stick to give her small child a whack on the head. She's clearly barmy. Strangely, however, no-one seems in the slightest bit perturbed by her behaviour.

Arrive in Jamaica, where all eyes are on Dean Headley. His dad Ron was born here and played for Jamaica and West Indies, and his grandfather George was one of the great West Indies figures. Dean was born in the West Midlands, after his father moved there and set himself up with Worcestershire, but he has loads of family on the island. On the bus ride to Kingston we sing, *'He's coming home, he's coming home. Deano's coming home'*. But he's a little nervous about what kind of reaction he's going to get here. He says he wants to keep a low profile, but as soon as we get to the hotel there is a queue of people outside waiting to shake his hands. We decide that the best policy is to take the piss slightly. For the moment he is seeing the funny side.

Friday 9 January

Sad start to the day with the news that David Bairstow, the ex-Yorkshire and England wicket-keeper, has committed suicide. Bumble played against him a fair amount for Lancashire and eight years ago he helped out on England's tour here by playing in one of the warm-up matches. Larger-than-life character, dead at 46. Has cricket got a higher suicide rate than other sports? Seems like it. David Frith, who used to edit *The Cricketer* and *Wisden Cricket Monthly,* filled a book with them. In Jack Russell's auto-biography he described a moment on the last tour here, when, after a bad day at the office, he stood on his balcony at the Pegasus in Georgetown and just had a little look over...

Second bit of bad news concerns Guyana, as it happens. The Canadian and British governments have now advised their citizens against travelling there, saying: 'Travellers should consider postponing non-essential travel until the situation returns to normal.' I feel a slight chill down the back of my neck. My mind goes back to our tour of India in 1993 when the destruction of a temple at Ayodhya resulted in hundreds of deaths. At Lucknow, the crowd for our match was swelled by 5,000 soldiers with rifles and we couldn't leave the hotel without an armed escort. Shortly before we were due to fly to Ahmedabad for a match, a pink-shirted official from the High Commission came to see us to assure us that 'Ahmedabad is perfectly safe. We are monitoring the situation closely.' The next day, while we were in mid-air going somewhere else, the Indian authorities announced they had called off the Ahmedabad match because they couldn't guarantee our safety. Everyone tries to reassure you that things will be okay, but sometimes you can't help feeling that you might be a little bit of a pawn in a chess game, an easy target for someone wanting to prove a point or make a name for their cause, or just some nutter with a gun.

When does travelling to a Test match become 'non-essential'? And who decides, by the way? Not us.

Talking of security, we are advised about dos and don'ts

in Kingston. Don't go too far from the hotel, don't go off on your own, do be sensible, do be streetwise, etc. Read in the newspaper that there were more than 1,000 murders in Jamaica last year. Comforting. There are definite no-go areas for us here. Introduced to Bob, our security man. Big bloke, Kingston copper, packs a piece which he calls his Amex because 'I don't leave home without it'. Tempted to ask how many he's downed, but his rather stern expression tells me I don't want to know.

Still can't get going as although we are here, our luggage is not. The customs people at the airport are holding up our 'coffins' and insisting on a thorough examination. Brian Murgatroyd, our press officer, is dispatched to the airport by our avuncular tour manager with the keys to open them up, goes about 25 yards and the front right wheel of his taxi drops off.

Unable to train, we go to Sabina Park to watch the first morning of the game between Jamaica and Barbados and to get first look at the re-laid pitch on which we are going to be playing the first Test match.

Hello. It looks VERY rough. Usually the surface is shiny enough for you to comb your hair in the reflection; this one looks like nothing I've ever seen before. It's bare, uneven and pitted with patchy grass, like a bad hair transplant that failed to take. Last winter, the West Indies Board got slated when their team played a series of boring matches against India on lifeless low pitches. Yes, they needed improving, but this does *not* look right. To make sure the pitch stayed together for this match, they watered it heavily. It is so damp that the start is delayed, but when play begins, jaws start to drop.

The odd ball flies off a length and almost every one jags off the seam. If this had happened back in England the pitch would have been considered unfit for first-classcricket and the home side docked 25 points, no worries. Embers spoke to Jeff Dujon and Mike Holding, both Jamaican,both West Indies greats. They are not impressed and warn that although the pitch for the Test match might be better than this, it will not be good. Will this change our strategy? Will they pick four pace bowlers? Will I get a game? Oh shit, here we go again. Decide to check my horoscope in Jamaica's daily paper, *The Gleaner*. 'Taurus: You should be most concerned with your professional accomplishments.' Decide not to check my horoscope again.

First experience of the Lara/Walsh thing. When we get back to the hotel some black Jamaican bloke comes up to Ashley Cowan and offers him $500,000 Jamaican (about £90,000) to get Lara out. Nice to see everyone is right behind the new skipper. It's still rumbling on. Loads of letters in the local papers plead with Walsh to stay. Unhelpfully for us, after winning the toss and sticking Barbados in to bat, Walsh takes six for 46 for Jamaica, as Barbados are bowled out for 135.

After getting back to the hotel, a few of us loosen up with a swim in the pool. I attempt to lift myself out of the water. Crunching pain. The wrist has gone again. With-out any bowling to remind myself of the problem, I have forgotten about it. Putting pressure on it in this way has caused it to collapse. Report to the physio, and he sets about organising a cortisone jab. Little bit of concern comes back.

Dean's first day going back to his roots was mixed. While he was having his picture taken round the back of the George Headley Stand, some local came up to him and said: 'Hey. Headley. You a white man.' Dean shrugged it off, then went to see the ground at Lucas CC where George played his first cricket back in the 1930s. The motto on the clubhouse wall is: 'To follow and yet to lead.' He's clearly moved by it all, but so far he is managing to keep his head on tight.

CHAPTER TWO

Angus Fraser, too old?

Saturday 10 January

PC Bob does the job. Part of his brief seems to be to make sure our bus gets to where it is going without the speedometer dropping below 50 mph. He leads the way to the Kensington Cricket Club for practice and, at the first sign of traffic, sticks the flashing blue light on top of his car. This is the signal for our bus driver, 'Goose' Mongoose, to boot the accelerator pedal through the floor. Flame on. We follow Bob's every move as he cuts a swathe through startled motorists slewing out of the way, and complete what should be a 25-minute journey in about eight.

On arrival, we discover a herd of goats on the outfield. Adam Hollioake, displaying some of his Captain Caveman characteristics, tries to round them up – to eat them, someone suggests.

Once they've been turfed off by the groundstaff, cricket at last. We opt for net practice in the middle, with pairs of batsmen batting for a set time or number of overs and the bowlers getting back into the swing. Try and have a bit of a bowl, to test out the wrist as much as anything. Not great. Not hurting badly, but I can feel it. It is getting in the way of normal bowling and also, to be honest, getting on my nerves.

Situation not helped when, backing up a throw at the stumps from Chalks, I narrowly avoid a ball that kicks off a stone straight at my head. I duck. Everyone wets themselves. Par for the course. That'll do, thanks, I'm off.

Watching the rest of the boys from the comparative safety of the caged-in pavilion, I flick through the pen pictures of the England squad provided in Sky television's media package. Some of the boys not best pleased e.g. 'DEAN HEADLEY: Another injury-prone English bowler...' ADAM HOLLIOAKE: His bowling with its subtle lack of pace could be vital...'

What *can* you say or write about Jack Russell? This is the first time we have managed to work out in the hot Caribbean sun. We're all wearing light training gear and shorts and we're still sopping wet with sweat and gasping for water, and there is Jack wearing fleece-lined tracksuit bottoms, two pairs of shirts and what look like diving boots on his feet. Those who have been with him on a few tours are used to his eccentricity by now. Anyone coming across him for the first time must be thinking: 'Who *is* this nutter?'.

Events brought to an early close by more sodding rain. Get back to the hotel and go straight to see physio Wayne Morton. He says that someone is coming to collect me to take me to the hospital for an X-ray on the wrist.

Now, I love the people who work in them, but I hate hospitals. The antiseptic smell makes me sick to my stomach. And the places scare me. To borrow a phrase, every corridor I look down is a corridor of uncertainty. My fear of hospitals is totally irrational, but it's there and there's nothing I can do about it.

Finally, we reach the X-ray room which is something out of *Tales From The Dark Side*. Hanging from the ceiling is this huge machine that wouldn't be out of place at the London

28

Planetarium. Scattered around the shelves are such luxury medical items as a cracked chamber pot and a false arm, the sight of which does little for my peace of mind.

Some bloke walks in wearing sandals and shorts and Wayne challenges him with: 'Who the hell are you?'. Turns out he's X-ray man.

Smile, please and off we go to see the surgeon. He looks at the pictures and we all agree nothing is broken. I've had cortisone before and it has worked before. It should work now. But we won't know until we try. If it doesn't work, God knows. *'Going Home. He's Going Home. Tufnell's going home'?*

Try a bit of bravado. Last thing I say to the doctor just as he is priming the needle is, 'Can I drink with this stuff inside me.' Wayne assures me that if I'm a brave boy, he'll let me have couple of rum and gingers. Fire away, I say, but deep down I am uneasy.

Return to the hotel with my arm strapped inside my shirt looking like Napoleon Bonaparte. Nasser nearly falls off his chair and is convinced I must be out of the tour. Shrug it off, but the thought that I might have come all the way out here for nothing is pissing me off. I sleep only in bits and pieces.

Sunday 11 January

Wake and immediately test wrist to see how it feels. Not too bad, but the real examination will come when I bowl. Not today, though.

Before embarking on Day Two of the Wyndham Hotel to Kensington CC rally, I ring home to let Lisa know what is happening. Things are improving a bit there. First couple of days of the tour, Poppy was poorly and, according to Lisa, looking around to see where I was. But she's a bit more settled now. Also, she has two teeth and, when prompted, says 'Dadadadadadada' down the phone. All a bit gooey, I know, but these phone calls home don't half make a difference sometimes.

When you see your name on Ceefax the day the squads are announced, there is no feeling like it. But the second thing that happens is that you look around the house at your wife and baby and think that's three months away from a life I rather like. I'm not complaining. This is the job I do. No-one is going to put food on your plate for nothing.

Spend the day at Kensington in dogsbody role, fetching water for the bowlers and batsmen. It is boiling out there. Chat to Bob about the level of crime in Kingston and he tells me that, with very few exceptions, there is danger on almost every corner. 'This place all right?' I enquire, fingering the bars of the steel cage around the pavilion. 'Oh yes,' he says, 'this is neutral territory. Everyone loves the cricket.' Just as well.

In one corner of the ground sits a group of locals, cricket-mad, knowledgeable and with an opinion on everything. They are, in turn, vociferous, then quietly absorbed. When Jack bats they call out: 'No, Russell! You jammin' it, like Bob Marley. You got to beat it, like Michael Jackson.' When Gussie bowls, they call out: 'Fraser! You bowling like a cow. You ready for milking.' As I stroll past them a couple are having a friendly chat about the relative merits of Carl Hooper (Guyana) and Jimmy Adams (Jamaica). They ask me: 'Tufnell … Who better, Hoops or Jimmy?' I put on my best diplomatic face. 'Well,' I say, 'they're both very good players. But perhaps Hooper is slightly more of an attacking batsman …' to which they have absolutely GONE OFF.

I pick up the pace of my stroll somewhat while scouring the ground for any sign of Bob. By the time I reach the pavilion they are still shouting at the top of their voices. Might possibly keep my mouth shut from now on.

End the day watching a shedload of American television. Intrigued by a trailer on the Home Box Office channel for a new series called *The Best Of Autopsy*. Sounds nice. 'Who says dead men tell no tales?' Can't wait.

Monday 12 January

Crunch-time for the wrist. Feels all right to have a bowl. Wayne has left it up to me, so here goes. First ball feels a little bit creaky. Second, a little easier. Third … what injury?

HUGE weight off my mind. Celebrate after practice with a few r and gs, but nothing untoward. Interestingly, in general the boys are a little more subdued in the soft drinks department than I recall from four years ago, or come to think of it from any previous tour I've been on. Talking of a different approach to fitness, I even caught myself doing a few sly sit-ups in front of the telly the other night. Me. Philip Tufnell. Doing sit-ups in front of the telly. With my reputation? Not sure I ought to spread that round too much. Next thing you know it'll be the Phil Tufnell Workout Video.

News that our scorer Malcolm 'Big Mal' Ashton has pulled off a major sponsorship deal with Pilot pens, who have agreed to keep him in stationery for the trip. In return he has has to smear Pilot stickers all over his coffin. Top man, Mal, and apart from being one of the men on whom Bennett regularly tests out his immense powers of delegation, he is the editor of *The Thrutcher*, an occasional newsletter for the amusement of the boys.

Issue 2, just out, carries the following item:

"Atherton in Smile Mystery: Our much awaited report on this most unusual phenomena is bogus!! A report that the Captain was seen smiling last week proved to be a complete falsehood. Apparently the skipper was suffering from a bad case of wind."

First match coming up against Jamaica at Jarrett Park, Montego Bay, starting Friday. On top of all the other concerns about arrangements and conditions etc., we now hear that there is a to-do brewing over the pitch in Mo Bay. Apparently, having decided that we must play the match there, on the other side of the island from Kingston, the Jamaican Cricket Board has held up the funds to get the pitch and outfield ready in time. Television pictures have shown it in a right state and Steve Bucknor, the Test umpire, has been sent up there to try and sort things out. We're trying to put such things of our minds, but the words 'effing shambles' have been circulating freely. We shall see.

Tuesday 13 January

Report in *The Gleaner* states that Courtney has made up his mind to carry on, even quoting him as saying: 'I am looking forward to the first Test against England, but I also wish that the controversy which has developed over the captaincy will end now. My aim first and foremost is to play Test cricket whether or not I am the captain, as that is the real issue.' Later he denies the report, claiming he was misquoted (so it happens here as well), but I get another reminder of the forces at work here when a taxi driver tells me: 'When you see Lara here for the Test match, tell him to get his ass off the island.'

The West Indies Board must be a little concerned as to what would happen if Walsh packed up now. The Jamaican crowd are notorious for getting stuck in if they feel that one of theirs has been badly done by. When Richie Richardson took over the job from Viv, the selectors decided to get rid of all the senior players including Jeffrey Dujon, Jamaican hero. Richie's first match in charge was a one-day international against South Africa at Sabina Park. The crowd held him personally responsible and booed him all the way to the wicket and every time he touched the ball.

Today we go to Sabina Park for our first practice session there. The nets are not yet ready, surprise, surprise, so we just do some stretching and catching. Take a look at the pitch just used for Jamaica's match with Barbados, the one the Test match will be played on in two weeks and two days' time. What can you say? It looks like a desert, a sandy surface with patches of scrub. Bumble's making all the right noises about how pleased we are with the facilities, probably mindful of the slagging off we got in Zimbabwe last year when we were criticised for moaning and not getting on with it. But it is fair to say that, with only two matches to play before the first Test, and whatever the reasons, we are not quite where we should be.

Dinner at Dover House, an old colonial-style restaurant in the middle of Kingston. The descriptions of the dishes in the menu are magnificent. I settle for 'a prime cut of contented beef', until the waiter informs me that it is not available. Presumably a bit too pissed off.

Wednesday 14 January

Tomorrow we travel to Montego Bay, some flying, some driving. I must be getting better as I opt for the eighteen minutes in the air as opposed to three-and-a-half hours on a coach squeaking and swerving around steep and paperclip-bend mountain roads. The trip is meant to be very picturesque, through the Blue Mountains and all that, but Dean, who has done it before, advises that there are some right lunatics up there who drive first and ask questions later.

Go to the ground for more running around. Courtney is there giving a press conference to confirm that he is going to carry on. He announces: 'I had to answer some questions for myself. I did not know if I still had the appetite for the game so I had to find out.' Oh, well. Can't win them all.

Our thoughts are turning to the make-up of the side for the first match. With so little cricket we will have to play the Test XI and that means some major disappointment for one or two of the guys. Once the tour really gets going, there will be very little opportunity, perhaps none, for the fringe players to get a game. Quite possible more than one will not play a match all winter.

I'm pretty sure that Athers came out here with it in mind to play both spinners, myself and Crofty, if the opportunity arose, and conversations in Antigua confirmed that. But if the Sabina Park pitch plays like it looks, i.e. crap, we might both be surplus to requirements. If they pick one of us, who's it going to be? People tell me I'm the man in possession after the final Test against the Aussies at The Oval, but, as I have learnt from experience, possession is only nine-tenths of the law. Until I'm out there on the field, I'm not out there on the field. If you see what I mean.

Thursday 15 January. Kingston to Montego Bay

Check in to the Sandals Resort in Mo Bay, as in Sandals on runway 23. Talk about conveniently situated within easy reach of the airport – if I lean out of my bedroom window I can pull the chocks away.

Repair to the beach until the other boys arrive and, while minding my own business catching forty winks on the beach, am startled out of my role in the latest Schwarzenegger blockbuster by the end of the world. Open my eyes to see an Air Jamaica 707 screaming over my head by a matter of inches.

The way the holiday-makers react to this event is peculiar, to say the least. To a man and woman, they all jump up and

34

wave frantically at the plane, whooping and hollering their approval. Please shut up. The first fly-past is bad enough. Little did I know, however, that this happy scene was to be re-enacted every hour on the half hour throughout the duration of our stay.

This is another all-inclusive pub, with all the benefits that implies, ahem. But it is also couples-only, which is a bit harsh on the boys. Everywhere you look people are kissing, cuddling, holding hands and gazing into each other's eyes, while sixteen blokes stand around in training gear feeling like pork chops at a barmitzvah. (Are you reading this, Lisa?)

The first serious business of the tour takes place in the evening, with a meeting where the team for tomorrow's match is to be announced and plans discussed. We're called into a function room for 7pm, but by this time Athers has already been among the chaps telling everyone whether they're in or out. This is something he instigated a couple of years back after recalling his own experience on the 1993 tour to India when he seemed to be out in the cold and never quite found out why. He doesn't like people learning they've been left out only when he announces the XI and I prefer it that way as well. There's nothing worse than just turning up at a team meeting, listening to the names being read out and not hearing yours. This way, if necessary, you're given a bit of time to get over your disappointment and it also avoids the slim but unsavoury prospect of some poor sod breaking down in tears in front of his colleagues and/or trashing the room, screaming 'YOU'LL PAY FOR THIS, YOU BASTARDS!'.

Sorry, got a bit carried away there.

The team is: Atherton, Stewart, Crawley, Hussain, Thorpe, Hollioake, Russell, Caddick, Headley, Fraser and Tufnell.

There is usually one guy who you consider unlucky not to make the cut. This time it's Ramps. Having replaced Creeps for the Oval Test, he made a solid 48 that helped us make what turned out to be a match-winning score, and he must have thought he would be given first crack out here. I feel for him a lot as he is my mucker and I've been there before myself.

This is the thing that he's been focusing on ever since the squad was announced back in September. Knowing Ramps he would have lived, breathed, eaten and slept this tour from that day forward, planning how he was going to play against Courtney and Curtly, how he was going to pace his batting, where he would be looking to score his runs, etc. – it would have shut out virtually everything else from his thoughts. Then he gets out here and it's sorry, mate, we can't fit sixteen players into eleven places. You know it's a team effort and all that, but in the actual moment you are told you're not playing I'm afraid the only bloke you are thinking of is yourself. That may not sound very good, but it's true. I'm in, thank god for that. Oh sorry, mate, you out? Human nature. And then, on a tour like this with so little cricket between the Test matches, for Ramps and the others left out – Crofty, Mark Butcher, Chris Silverwood, Ashley Cowan – comes the realisation that you might actually not get a game at all. However you try to frame it, three months sitting on your backside or ferrying drinks around for other people and showing what a good tourist you are is no-one's idea of what they are here for.

Tea, coffee and a few beers available and the meeting follows the usual pattern. Athers reads out the list, then he, Bumble and Embers have a chat about what we're doing, tactics and some specific technical stuff about the players we're up against. (Courtney has taken the game off, which, bearing in mind what we have been told about the pitch, we are all gutted about). As for the conditions we are likely to be facing, there is a general feeling that we are not going to be playing on too many flat ones all tour. So far, each time we drive past or visit a Test ground as at St John's in Antigua or Sabina Park, all we hear is that the pitch is being or has been re-laid. Nothing we can do about it, no-one is moaning, but such things do tend to get into people's heads. If you're facing two of the best fast bowlers in the world, both having taken well over 300 Test wickets and both releasing the ball from about nine feet, it helps if you're not doing it on a minefield.

Afterwards I go and see Ramps and have a little chat, coming up with all the usual old cobblers about keeping his head up, 'things may change', etc. But I've heard that from other people when I've been the odd man out and it never makes any difference. Personally I'm surprised he's not in, but the selectors have to back their hunch. He's cut up and that's that. The bottom line is that, no matter how you are told, or how logical the reasons behind the decision being made might be, you just feel as though someone has ripped your arse out.

What is important is we all rally round the guys who aren't included.

Afterwards we repair for a nightcap and wade straight into every cricketer's worst nightmare – an American who wants to learn about cricket.

'Gee. Are you guys with the team?'

'Yes.'

'Cricket. That's kinda like baseball ain't it.'

'No.'

'Sure it is. You got the batters and the catchers and the pitchers like we do.'

'No. We haven't.'

'Sure you do. And I've seen that poem about when you're out you're in and the next man's out and then he's in and then the team that's been in goes out and the team that's been out goes in. And tell me why is England always losing.'

'Excuse me. We are having a private chat. We don't mean to be rude but would you mind...?'

'Mind what?'

'Go away.'

'I don't wanna. I don't wanna...'

God I hope the game never catches on over there.

Before kipping, ring home. Lisa tells me Poppy now has four teeth. Don't know why, but this sticks in my mind all night.

Friday 16 January, Jamaica v England

Topping start to the day for Bumble. He relates to us the story of his morning wake-up call. The phone in his room rings at 5.45 am. On the other end is a reporter from IRN radio, calling from London, who mumbles something Bumble can't hear or understand and then asks: 'What did you have for breakfast?' Bumble replies: 'What did I have for breakfast? It's a quarter to six in the sodding morning.' The voice says, 'I'm sorry David, but I think we had better start the interview again'. Second question: 'Well, David, thanks for joining us. How is the first Test going?'. Third question: 'Angus Fraser, best bowler in England?'. Fourth question: 'Angus Fraser, too old?'. Finally Bumble apologises that the line is terrible and puts the phone down.

Arrive at the ground to discover that the outfield and pitch are not bad, as we have been led to believe. They are ten times worse. The outfield is like a theme park, comprising a host of attractions for the active holiday-maker. Here is Swamp

Land, where you can watch your loved ones being sucked underground by the cloying mud. Or why not try Savannah Land, where you can stalk your prey undetected in the long grass? And here is everybody's favourite – Ant Land. Watch them scuttle about under you feet, then make moving patterns up and down your leg. See how many of the little mites you can squash before they bite the crap out of you.

Funny how, not having played a game of cricket since September, you slip back so easily into the pre-match routine. In the dressing room the ghetto blaster is put on and the boys start rucking about the choice of sounds. Find a spot to park my backside, as usual when we're in the side together, right next to Creeps so we can nick fags off one another. Always seems to be that one of us is out of smokes. Trot off for the warm-up, cursing that last cigarette, then join in a prolonged and fevered discussion over how the pitch is going to play. As per normal, the seamers think it's going to turn square and the spinners are convinced it will seam all over the place.

Only one thing is sure: it's a slagheap. And on the basis that it will only get worse, when Athers wins the toss, the decision is to bat first.

I am a notoriously bad watcher. Contrary to popular opinion, that's not because I'm not interested, but because I get too involved. 'Shot, come on, come on there's one there, run, run ... no, NO, get back, GET BACK!! JEEESUS CHRIST...' Normally after about five minutes of this, one of the batsmen will tell me to shut up or piss off, or both, at which point I will slink off to a quiet corner for a nap.

This being the first match of the tour, I resolve to sit and watch quietly.

Against quite a lively attack on a damp and dodgy pitch, we get our first reminder of what batting out here can be like;

namely all lovely, lovely for a while, then, in a matter of seconds, Armaggedon.

Alec goes early, then Athers and Creeps put on fifty-odd, all nice and tidy, so we're 52 for one at lunch. Well done, boys, keep it going. Twenty minutes later we're 78 for four – Athers, Creeps and Nasser back in the hutch and memories come racing back of last winter in Zimbabwe when we lost our first game of the tour to Mashonaland and the brown stuff hit the ventilation appliance big time. Fortunately, Chalks then proceeds to bat like the little master he can be and Adam 'Smokes' Hollioake blasts a quick 40 to get us back on track. Reach the close with Chalks 74 not out after four hours of grinding it out.

Get back to the hotel and realise that although I have done nothing all day I am absolutely knackered. What's it going to be like when I'm running around in this heat, not just sitting around in it?

An interview has been set up by Vodafone, one of our sponsors, with a reporter called Robert Crampton, to appear in the Weekend section of *The Times*. I am not overly keen because I always seem to end up talking about the same old stuff to people who act as though they've known me for years … but these things have to be done, I suppose. I spend about twenty minutes with the bloke back at the hotel. Seems all right. I just hope he doesn't want to make a tosser of me like some have tried to do in the past. He goes on about social 'class' a bit too much for my liking, but as Vodafone have paid for him to come out here with a photographer, I presume his approach will be positive. We shall see. They want me to go off to a beach for some photos at about 7.30 on Sunday morning. Bit early if you ask me, especially as we will be right in the middle of the match. There you go, all part of the service.

Saturday 17 January

Getting the feel of real Caribbean cricket now. In one corner of the ground is a stack of speakers blaring out loud music, erupting with sound whenever the opposition take a wicket or score a boundary; in another, a rastafarian selling coconut water, in coconuts. These he opens up for the customers by slicing off the top with a very sharp and very long machete. There are peanut sellers everywhere and LOTS of general noisiness.

Chalky bats on, finally out after six-and-a-half hours, then we declare at 286 for eight, so the moment of my first bowl is coming closer. Not for a while though, because the pitch is perfect for our quicks. Dean Headley gets his first taste of what is likely to be in store for him when, just as he is running up to bowl his opening ball on tour, the speakers deafen us with 'DEAN HEADLEY, GRANDSON OF THE LEGENDARY GEORGE HEADLEY', stopping him dead in his tracks. So much for a low profile. Fortunately for him, he bowls spot on and takes our first three wickets of the tour which helps him relax. He's been under a bit of pressure and it's important that he shows quickly that he is more than just a name here, and he has done. He's chuffed.

My turn, briefly. Nice to get out there and have a fight at last. Too many no-balls really, probably because having to run through a cowfield to get to the crease is making me strain too hard to get there, but have a stroke of luck when Jimmy Adams, the Test player, cuts a ball from me onto his stumps. Caddy then tears into them and they end up struggling at 101 for eight.

While watching the seam bowlers do the damage I am distracted by a series of messages from the bloke on the PA asking for two cars to be removed. 'Please do so as no-one wants to get the constabulary involved,' he advises. As time goes on his mood becomes darker until finally he announces: 'To the owners of the cars mentioned before, I have to inform you that the vehicles are now on fire.'

Sunday 18 January

Rise bright and early to do the pics for *The Times* interview then get to the ground. If we finish them off quick first time, the plan is to get them to follow on and try and win the game rather than use the match for batting practice. This is sensible because batting on this kind of surface is no practice for anyone. Uneven bounce, some going upwardly-vertical, some going underground, means this is the worst first-class pitch I have ever played on.

We do the job and I get into some kind of rhythm, taking another four for 33. But the farcical nature of the business is emphasised by the fact that when Jack stands up to the stumps for my bowling, he keeps wicket in a helmet with a full face visor. He managed to see well enough to give me a first in cricket – the first stumping off my bowling by a keeper in a hard hat. My victim is Robert Samuels. Another first in my career as a professional cricketer is that we employ a long-stop to field directly behind Jack for the quick bowlers. Angus is deputed to perform that function but when one ball scoots under Jack then hits a stone and bounces past the big man as well, there is general falling about. We call for a long stop for the long stop.

Rohan Kanhai, the former West Indies Test batsman and now the coach of Jamaica, summed up everyone's feelings. 'There is no way a first-class match should have started on this pitch. It was just not a cricket wicket.'

More seriously, Gus appears to be 'reaching' a bit. While the other pace bowlers are running though the opposition on a helpful pitch, Gus doesn't seem to be making much impression. Having apparently been selected mainly as back-up for Darren Gough, Headley and Caddick, Darren's injury means Gus is now one of our front-line bowlers and for that to work he has to perform. He'll be okay, we hope, but he hasn't played a Test for two years and it is asking a lot.

Anyway, we win easily half an hour before tea on the third day and stop off on the way back to the hotel at a bar called Margeuriteville to celebrate with some mucking about down the waterchute. At the bottom of this is a floating platform on which we perform some WWF tag wrestling. I'm thrown off in seconds.

CHAPTER THREE

Tufnell in 'three-in-a-bedroom romps'

Monday 19 January. Montego Bay to Kingston

Late night, thick head.

Very odd story from Margeuriteville concerning Crofty and Creeps and a sea urchin, of which, via *The Thrutcher*, more anon. The newsletter also publishes the latest instructions from Simon Pack, our newly-appointed International Teams Director. Former commander-in-chief of allied forces in the Med. or some such, very fine upstanding figure and all that. His idea is to introduce personal development plans for the players which can only be a good thing. But the 'familiarisation' session organised for the boys prior to departure regarding information about the West Indies went a bit awry.

The Thrutcher gives us Simon's latest missive, thus:

On Manouevres with Simon Pack:
'This is the Major-General speaking to you from HQ.
    Stand easy, smoke 'em if you've got 'em.
    Now boys. Just want you to know. This tour, no pushover. Here to give our commonwealth cuzzins a taste of their own medicine, 'cos they don't like it up 'em!

Familiarisation talk at Copthorne, bit of a cock-up. Buffet excellent. Russell! Get that 'air trimmed, lad! And any more lip from you Morton and it's the glasshouse – 30 days with drill.

Have cancelled all transport from Montego Bay to Kingston. Party will be given 24 hours to yomp, full pack, back to Kingston. Anyone not making it in time will be sent on an intensive course into the working of the Duckworth/Lewis method (note: D/L method is the totally unfathomable new system for devising new targets for one-day matches in the event of rain).

'In the meantime – Diiiis-missed.'

We depart a day ahead of schedule after finishing off the match in three days and head back to Kingston. Day off. Sleep heavily.

Tuesday 20 January

First Courtney, now Curtly. There is a report in *The Gleaner* claiming that Ambrose is set to retire. Er, yes, please. 'A source close to the fast bowler told the Caribbean News Agency (CANA) that Ambrose has already written his retirement letter, in which he says he has been considering his future for the past few weeks.' The boys are not taking this too seriously at the moment but my mind goes back to a conversation with a barman at the Jolly Harbour in Antigua straight after Lara was appointed captain. He told me that Amby and Lara do *not* get on. The problem, he claims, goes back to the 1995 West Indies tour of England when Lara was perceived by the Antiguan boys, Richie Richardson, Ambrose and Kenny and Winston Benjamin, to have been leading a dressing-room coup against Richie, the captain. This bloke tells me that when the infighting reached its worst point, Amby actually took Lara to one side and suggested that Lara's face and Curtly's fist might make a perfect match.' Don't know about any of that, but bearing in mind how many times he has given us strife in the past, we are somewhat dubious that Amby is willing to pass up the opportunity of another crack.

Back in Kingston becoming increasingly aware of the amount of hustling going on around our hotel. Big drugs problem here has created subculture of desperation. One bloke with eyes like pools of mud regularly comes up to me, demanding money. We have been told to walk on by, but some of them keep coming. God knows how you deal with all this. Perhaps my most distressing experience of beggars was in India on the 1993 tour. Made light of it with my famous, or infamous foot-in-mouth comment: 'Done the poverty, done the elephants' – well done, Tuffers – but it got me every time. Women barely in their mid-teens carrying babies in one arm and holding out the other. Some of them look so completely beaten up by the life they lead that you feel like handing over everything. Makes you realise just how lucky you are. Then again, the wrong kind of charity can cause problems as well. I was told by one of the journos about an incident in which one of them was involved in his first trip to India. When his taxi stopped at a traffic light in the middle of Calcutta, some poor kid in rags knocked on the window and held out his hand. The journo reached for his wallet, pulled out a 500 rupee note (a few bob in our terms, but REAL money to these people) and as the car pulled away from the lights he dropped it out of the car. He turned around to see if the kid collected the note, only to see the most almighty scrap develop from nowhere. Twenty or thirty kids punching and kicking the crap out of each other for a couple of quid. Carnage. You even hear stories of mothers mutilating their own kids so as to make them more 'valuable' in the begging market.

Wednesday 21 January

Cancel that gold watch for Curtly. Today's edition of *The Gleaner* carries the West Indies squad for our first Test at Sabina Park starting next Thursday, and Amby is in. The paper says he describes the stories about his riding off into the sunset as 'vicious rumours'. Lara's first squad has no real surprises and he tells reporters: 'I promise the people of the Caribbean that, although I have had my indiscretions, I have thought long and hard about what I intend to do in the future and that those days are behind me'. Brian Lara. Captain of West Indies. World record holding best left-handed batsman in the world. Indiscretions? With his reputation?

Trot down to Sabina Park for nets and practice. The nets are not great but what does that Test pitch look like? Eight days to go and it is still a desert with bits of scrub plonked down at irregular intervals. And it looks bumpy. Athers tries to be positive and the message is: 'Don't worry. It will play better than it looks.' Not terribly convinced. No point worrying about it, but Courtney and Curtly will be licking their lips. Slight fracas when fielding practice starts and I am still in the Kingston CC pavilion shovelling down some chicken and rice. Sorry, boys, missed breakfast.

In the corner of the ground under the scoreboard, workmen are putting the final touches to the Sandals beach. They're going to lay down sand and a swimming pool and supply punters with as much grog as they can swill for J$500 a day. Hope the bikini-clad lovelies don't present too much of a distraction for the boys fielding at fine leg, or is this part of a sinister plot by the West Indies Board to put us off our stroke?

On return journey, notice the sheer variety of items available to motorists from street-corner sellers; usual stuff like newspapers, chunks of pineapple etc., but also more exotic goods like individual electric plug sockets. At one set of traffic lights some bloke was selling ironing boards.

Thursday 22 January, West Indies 'A' v England, Chedwin Park

To Chedwin Park, about 45 minutes from Kingston (25 mins with Bob, again causing carnage) to play four-day game against West Indies 'A'. Respect to Jamaica and all that, but this will be more of a challenge than last week's match as they are a stronger side. Nixon McLean, young fast bowler named in the Test squad, and Reon King, young and faster bowler from Guyana, are touted in advance as 'Thunder and Lightning' by Joel Garner. I make a point of not arguing with Joel Garner as he is 12ft tall and still quick. The side is being led by Roland Holder, dangerous batsman with a point to prove after being dropped by the Test selectors after their tour to Pakistan.

Our selection is interesting. Dean is having it off, as they say, following his run out at Jarrett Park, and our selectors – Athers, Bumble, Nasser, as vice-captain and our assistant coach John Emburey – have decided to let Ashley Cowan have a crack alongside Gus. English media have built this up as a sort of head-to-head between the old stager and the young tyro. Don't exactly see it that way, because I think Gus is sure to play in the first Test come what may. In fact ten of the XI we pick: Atherton, Stewart, Crawley, Hussain, Thorpe, Hollioake, Russell, Caddick, Fraser and Tufnell – plus Headley, is the team we expect will start the Test next week. But Bumble gives everyone something to think about when he says in advance that if Ash bowls well he will come

Athers, Butch and Ash, with me, Phil Tufnell, on my second tour of the West Indies. With *my* reputation?

Above: England players ready to do business out in the Caribbean … Er, manager where's the bus?

Below: Masterblaster II? Mali Richards, son of the great Viv, meets Athers in Antigua at the start of the tour. Note the rain clouds starting to build on the horizon.

Happiness is a worn gun. While in Kingston before the start of the
first Test, I rarely strayed far from pistol-packing bodyguard
Bob Wedderburn.

Dean Headley, on his first Caribbean tour, no doubt anticipating the heavy workload ahead on the beach at the Jolly Harbour, Antigua.

Mark Butcher (right) chose between cricket and music for a career. After his first ball at Sabina Park, he might have been thinking twice. Here he is accompanied by Bob Marley and John Crawley.

'All present and correct for practice at Sabina Park, sir, except … where's Tufnell?' Trying to shovel down a late breakfast of jerk chicken, rice and peas in the Kingston CC pavilion bar, as it happens.

Preparing to face the music from Curtly and Courtney ... or is that Nasser Hussain modelling the latest cricket collection from Vivienne Westwood? Very nice.

England v West Indies 'A' at Chedwin Park, Kingston. Dropping Roland Holder off my own bowling – not a very auspicious prelude to the main course.

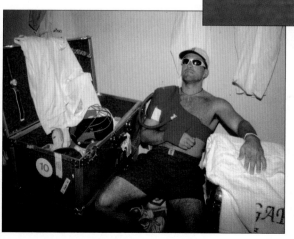

Adam Hollioake looking glum but winning the battle to get his shoulder fit for the first Test at Sabina Park.

There are people on the pitch ... they think it's all over. It was. The Sabina Park experiment to stage a Test match on a pitch made of moon rock was deemed only a qualified success.

'Where haven't you hit me, Curtly ...' Alec Stewart shows his disgust after being pummeled by Ambrose for the umpteenth time. Soon after, the captains convened and the match was called off.

John Crawley cuts Dennis Rampersad during England's game against Trinidad and Tobago at Guaracara Park. I was left at home in Port-of-Spain for fear my fags might blow us all to Kingston come.

Above: Another suitcase in another airport lounge. Jack Russell, Alec Stewart and physio Dean Riddle wait for another flight.

Below: Thorpey taking time off from dodging the bouncers to write home from the comfort of his hotel room.

The England party in their best gear at the Queen's Park Oval, Port-of-Spain. At least I had the right clothes this time.

into contention. Little bit of pressure on Gus and this wicket looks like it will be a batter's paradise.

This tour is a huge challenge for the big man. He hasn't played a Test match since Uncle Ray showed him the door when we lost to South Africa in Cape Town, and has spent the intervening period bending the ears of the Middlesex boys with the information them that England have been barmy not to pick him.

Have to admit there was a certain amount of surprise in our dressing-room when he was selected, not because we didn't think he could do a job, but because it looked as though he might have taken up permanent residence on the international scrapheap. As things turned out, he is now a front-line bowler here and a key part of the plan. Leaving sentiment aside, if he is bowling well, he is the right kind of bowler for this place as he puts the ball in what used to be called the 'corridor of uncertainty', and which people have now taken to describing as the 'business area', which basically means he doesn't bowl crap, and usually makes the batsmen play him. His personal duel with Lara goes back a long way. Those who attended any of his benefit functions last season can now go and put the kettle on, but his favourite after-dinner story is worth repeating for anyone who hasn't yet heard it. Lord's 1995, second Test, England v. West Indies. Gus, left out of the first Test, comes back with revenge in his heart and bowls one which holds its line against the slope and gets inside Lara's forward push. Howzaaat? Dead lbw. Gus's 100th Test wicket. He retires to his fielding station on the boundary, feeling somewhat pleased with himself. 'I wasn't expecting a standing ovation,' he says, 'but I thought I might get a round of applause'. So when some bloke calls out 'Oi, Fraser', he pumps himself up to receive the compliment, then hears: 'Tosser. What did you do that for? I paid thirty-five quid to watch Lara bat, not to watch you bowl all day.'

There's been no better professional on the circuit and no better mate to me. But we're none of us getting any younger and he knows this is his last chance. We're pulling for him but Test cricket, as he knows, is no place for personal feelings. If he isn't bowling well, he won't play, same for all of us. They've picked Ashley for a reason. Can't really tell if this is getting to Gus. He's showing no outward signs of anxiety, but then he rarely does.

We lose the toss and are stuffed in. Thunder and Lightning live up to their advance billing and in no time we are 30 for three. Oh, shit. Here we go again.

Or do we? Barmh … barmh … barmh…

As we are all well aware, this is the kind of situation that playing out here is all about. But, just as the 'duffers' headlines are being dusted off again back home, Nass and Chalks produce a superb partnership of 184. Thorpey is out for 81, but Nass finishes the day 131 not out, with young Smokes 33 not out.

The Test match is a week away today and interest is brewing in Kingston, but the real deal as far as the locals are concerned appears to be the story of the Reggae Boyz. The Jamaican football team has emulated the *Cool Runnings* success of their Olympic bobsleigh counterparts by qualifying for the World Cup finals for the first time. They have a big match against Brazil coming up in a couple of weeks and will warm-up for that with a game against Sweden in Kingston on the night of the first day of the Test match at Sabina. The people here are as curious to know what we think of the Boyz as they are about the cricket. Diplomatically, I forecast at least a World Cup quarter-final place for their brave lads, which seems to be the right answer.

Another trailer for *The Best Of Autopsy* claims: 'A DNA sample tells a thousand words.' I am REALLY looking forward to this.

Friday 23 January

News reaches us of the press conference given by Geoff Boycott back home regarding his conviction and sentencing in a French court after they believed the story of his ex-lover Margaret Moore, that he beat her up. Coincidentally the local *Weekend Observer* newspaper reports that Boycott has been invited to play in a match between the Jamaican and English media. 'Should Boycott play,' it states, 'he stands the chance of assaulting the ball only...'

Chedwin Park, Day Two. Nass bats on and the lower order get their chance of another hit, encouraging the PA announcer to demonstrate the full range of his descriptive powers. Hollioake is '*considered* to be an all-rounder', he tells us, Andy Caddick is 'a tall one', Ashley Cowan, who is making his first appearance for England, 'ain't done nothing yet'. I don't actually make it to the wicket as we declare on 400 for eight, but for some reason the voice decides I am worthy of a mention. He reads out my batting average, then, under his breath, mutters 'he had better be a bowler.' As usual the bloke is also kept busy with the bogus calls. Throughout the day there are urgent messages for Mr Hugh Jarse, Mr. Brandon Pickles, and Bumble's personal favourite, Terry Fie deVerk.

Gus eases any worries he might have had by cleaning up both openers but Holder settles in and plays well. By the close I have another wicket, bowling Keith Semple, and I should have had Holder, caught off the glove at silly point by Thorpey, but not given. Holder was 10 at the time. Hope that doesn't prove too costly, as he's 57 not out at the close from their 156 for three.

But the big story concerns Adam Hollioake. Semple has hit one from Gus like a tracer bullet into the covers, Smokes dives to field it and as he hits the hard outfield has just let out a little 'ow.' He gets up, races after the ball, picks it up and throws it in as though nothing has happened, then screams 'AH-AAAOOOOWWWW'. He's standing there like a racehorse that has just broken its leg, with his right arm stuck in a strange-looking position, locked forward and sort of flapping in the wind. Alec Stewart and me, who are the fielders nearest to him run over, tell him not to move and call for the physio Wayne Morton.

Wayne takes one look at him and realises that something has popped out and that he must try to pop it back in again, sharpish. He lays Smokes down on the deck, grabs hold of his right hand, sticks his foot on his chest, and yanks.

I'm not good with this kind of stuff. When they were handing out the pills marked courage in the face of physical pain, by the time I reached the head of the queue, they'd run out. So when I hear this crunching sound like someone has had a go on an old football rattle, I turn white and feel a peculiar sensation in the pit of my stomach. I manage to avoid becoming the first cricketer to faint while witnessing treatment being administered to a stricken colleague, but only just. Smokes is struggling, though, and leaves the field.

Too early to tell, but if the injury is as bad as it looked at first, this will be a big blow. He is due to start the first Test as our extra (fourth) seamer and number six, with instructions to make sure we don't get bogged down in the middle of our innings, which can happen all too easily out here.

Saturday 24 January

Skimming through the morning paper on the way to the ground, I can't help noticing that the bloke in the picture at the top of the personal's column looks remarkably like Dean Headley. Having had my attention snared, I read on.

HUMOROUS CHEF – with heart, mind and spirit to match. VERY HANDSOME and humble 6ft 2ins, seeking peaceful female.
SLIGHTLY DESPERATE Man, 6ft, easy-going, honest. Meet me on the football field or baseball court. Seeking that female who will literally captivate me with her charms.

Before play starts lots of speculation about Adam Hollioake. He tells reporters that he wanted to get back on the field straight after coming off, but as time went on, the pain told him that this was not something he was going to shrug off. After treatment he has his right arm put in a sling, but Wayne reckons he is better than 50–50 for the Test. The injury is not a full dislocation and if anyone is going to recover in time, it will be this bloke. Strong as a bull-elephant. Always going on about rounding up wild animals for a fight. Worrying thing is that he means it.

With one bowler short this turns into a long day. What did I say about Holder's escape not being too costly? Roland the Rat proceeds to make his career-best 183. Holder wanted to make a big one and showed no interest in Athers' offer of a declaration deal to make a game of it. As the pitch flattens out to a featherbed, we come to our first realisation of how physically tough this can be, fielding all day in the hot Caribbean sun, especially towards the end of a day when your mind can just slip out of gear.

We worked our butts off, but not much went for us. Ramps, on as a substitute fielder for Smokes, dropped one off Gus that was driven straight to him at cover. Cue the announcer, in mid-over, with: 'That one dropped by

53

Ramprakash, usually a very good fielder' which makes Ramps feel just peachy. Gus then bowls someone off a bastard no-ball. Lots of decent lbw shouts turned down which pisses everyone off. Then, in the last hour, McLean comes out and absolutely smashes it everywhere. One of those time-stands-still moments when Caddy gave him a very respectable bouncer and he swings it over the fence at mid-wicket, flat. Athers said it was one of the best shots he'd ever seen. Don't think we'll be bowling too many more short ones to young Nixon in future.

Sunday 25 January

Game peters out, but Gus and I are happy with our work, even though he doesn't show it. One of the great sights in cricket is watching Gus grunting and rucking, pink-faced with effort, kicking the ground when he bowls a bad ball, or gets hit for four ... or a catch is dropped off him, or he bowls someone off a no-ball ... Sorry, I'll stop smirking now.

Shame Holder didn't want to have a game, but I suppose his attitude is that this match was not put on for our benefit. Anyway he's proved his point, although the whole thing might have been different had he been given out when I thought I had him. I felt I bowled all right – four for 100-odd from seven point three million overs on a flat one. I'll settle for that.

Get back to the hotel. Very tired, but perk up with the prospect of Lisa's arrival here tomorrow. After three weeks apart, I'm looking forward to what the *Test Match Special* boys might call 'the champagne moment.'

Monday 26 January

Rest day starts badly. Sadistic team-mate or clerical error, I receive an unscheduled alarm-call at 5.45 am.

Vodafone have organised a golf day at the Caymanas course, a match between players and media. Thanks, but no thanks. Nothing against the press lads (in fact, I get on well with most, if not all), but I am shattered and the prospect of dragging my weary carcass around eighteen holes is about as appealing as bowling to Lara on a featherbed with no umpires or fielders present.

Later, Lisa arrives with her friend Claire. They are here for the duration of the first Test, which starts on Thursday. They know the score, but I can see that Lisa's presence here raises all the old questions about players' wives and girlfriends being with the boys on tour that no-one has yet resolved satisfactorily. Last year, when we were away in Zimbabwe and New Zealand, missing Christmas and away for the best part of four months, the rule was no wives or girlfriends and it was not, shall we say, universally popular. Also, prior to Lord MacLaurin's insistence that we all should have single hotel rooms on tour, in Harare, for instance, there were sixteen sweaty blokes squeezed into shoeboxes two at a time, hanging out their smalls and trying to conduct private telephone conversations with the ones they left behind while their room-mates were busy clipping their toenails. Now that's good for morale.

There are two schools of thought. Some say that the presence of visitors can take your mind off the job, some say that is no bad thing. But if you took the 'distraction' theme to its logical conclusion, no-one with a job would ever have a relationship. I think people make too much of a meal of it. Granted, sometimes the sheer numbers can get a little out of hand as they did, apparently, on the 1995–96 tour to South Africa when, in Cape Town, the party was swelled to the population of greater Los Angeles, but in the main, as long as people are sensible, there's no problem. If the girls and kids do break concentration and interfere with team spirit, then the concentration and team spirit must be pretty fragile in the first place.

As far as Lisa and Claire are concerned, they managed to get on a standby flight and just popped over for a week to sit by the pool and get a tan. In any case, the fact that the three of us are sharing accommodation is a positive boon to morale. The sight of me tottling up to Room 709 with two gorgeous females brings a little ray of sunshine into all our lives, provides material for hours of gossip along the lines of "Tufnell in three-in-a-bedroom romps" and a little fantasy release for the boys in those quieter moments. Me. Philip Tufnell. Escorting two lovely ladies to my hotel room for the night. With my reputation?

Seriously, it's nice for me and, I think, good for the chaps to have a little innocent female company around. Some favour the Australian method, if you'll pardon the expression, whereby when they come out here for a tour they set up a couple of friendly matches in Bermuda at the end of the trip. The families have a nice holiday together, the cricket is a winding-down, not-too-serious exercise and the Bermuda Cricket Board pays for the jolly. Memo to ECB: please investigate further.

The West Indies boys are arriving in dribs and drabs. Lara is in and no reports of riots yet. Letters in the local papers from disgruntled Jamaicans insist they will boo him when he goes on the field at Sabina Park on Thursday. But Courtney is making all the right noises about getting behind him and there is some suggestion that they will make a thing of the two guys shaking hands to try and nip in the bud any displays of dissent.

CHAPTER FOUR

'What the **** is going on?'

Tuesday 27 January

Two days to go before the Test match starts, and everyone is really revving up now. Lara is quoted in the papers as saying that the re-laid Sabina Park pitch holds no fears for him. David Graveney, our chairman of selectors, who has arrived here with his wife, joins us at the ground to take a look at the surface at practice.

We are all somewhat perturbed, to say the least. Although it looked terrible last week, the ground authorities assured us that it would be in good nick by the time we got back here. But it clearly is not. In fact it looks God awful.

There are dry, puffy cracks, shiny areas and tufts of bush grass. We roll a ball from end to end and halfway down it starts to bounce up and down the undulations. Even Athers, who normally tends to be upbeat whatever the conditions look like, is shocked. 'Christ,' he says, 'this looks dreadful.'

There are rumours circulating that Barry Jarman, the Australian match referee and the umpires Steve Bucknor and Venkat have already had preliminary discussions. Jarman, apparently, is very concerned. He is not the only one, I can assure you. I know it is the same for both sides, but we don't both have Courtney and Curtly. This does not look good.

One of the press guys is advised to have a little chat with the match officials just in case. He replies : 'No-one is interested in stories about the pitch.'

In the evening we attend an official function laid on by Cable and Wireless, the West Indies sponsors, to celebrate the start of the series. Meanwhile Dean's attempts to keep a low profile are becoming increasingly futile. Last night, along with Courtney, he was honoured with life membership of the Melbourne Cricket Club, the leading local club, and tonight everyone stands up and sings happy birthday to him.

Wednesday 28 January

Everything intensifies now. Practice at ground again. Playing surface looking a shade more like a cricket pitch, but not much. Smokes has a fitness test and he is all right to play. Extraordinary recovery, very strong bloke.

Main focus is on the team meeting. Athers, having gone through the usual procedure of letting everyone know whether they're in, reads out the XI. It is: Atherton, Stewart, Crawley, Hussain, Thorpe, Hollioake, Russell, Caddick, Headley, Fraser, Tufnell. The chat is reasonably straight-forward – hard lines to those who haven't made it etc., then discussion about how their batsmen play which reinforces what we have talked about before.

The pitch is discussed at length. According to Athers, at one point, the groundsman had laid a length of string from end to end down each edge of the pitch, in turn, to help his assistant cut the grass straight. On one side the string was touching the ground at certain points and at others it wasn't. Not exactly the *Oxford English Dictionary's* definition of the word 'flat'.

The message to our batsmen is that they must be positive. Very, very important not to lose the first Test of any series,

58

but bearing in mind recent history, particularly so out here. Four years ago we did, they then grabbed the initiative and before we knew it we were 3–0 down after three. Prior to the rain-affected draw with South Africa in the opening match of the 1995–96 series, England lost the first Test of the three preceding tours, to Australia, West Indies and India and finished up losing heavily each time, 3–1, 3–1 and 3–0. However the pitch actually plays, we can't believe there will not be a result here one way or another, and there almost always is in Trinidad where we play the second Test (last week the match there between Trinidad and Tobago and the Leeward Islands ended inside two days with Lara's side losing by ten wickets on a dodgy surface). So if one team gets the upper hand early on, the series could be won and lost in the space of two Tests in three weeks.

All this is followed by a screening of some motivational tapes provided by Sky television, showing each player's 'Greatest Hits' set to music. I watch myself bowling at The Oval to the soothing strains of Sid Vicious singing his version of *My Way*. I never get over looking at this strange, somewhat shambling creature bowling for England in Test matches who, so they say, is me.

The big idea behind these images is that they are supposed to help us when we are on the field to visualise our good performances or think through what is likely to happen in certain situations should we encounter them again. A lot of people pooh-pooh all this kind of stuff as 'psycho-babble', but I find it works well. If some bastard with a bat in his hand starts to take a liking to you and you begin to wonder what on earth you are doing out there, it doesn't half help to have handy a mental picture of yourself actually getting someone out.

After the team meeting, a quiet dinner and early bed.

Surprisingly relaxed, really, but as my Middlesex colleagues will no doubt verify, I never seem to have too much trouble getting to sleep. A few musings about tomorrow, including slight niggling concerns about their bowlers on that pitch.

Last conscious thought before I drop off: 'Duck.'

Thursday 29 January, First Test, Sabina Park, Day 1

Close of Play: England 17–3 after 10.1 overs (Stewart 9*, Thorpe 0*). Match abandoned.

WHAT was all that about?

The most bizarre day of my career. It starts normally enough: get up about 7.30, breakfast, leave the hotel in the Bob-led convoy at 8.15. Arrive at Sabina Park, 8.35-ish, ready for kick-off at 10am. However, by 2pm on the first afternoon of the first match of the 1998 test series between England and West Indies, we are back at the hotel pool, sipping cold beers.

The first bad omen concerns Jack Russell. While we are having breakfast the word goes round that he is not feeling great – in fact, since the night of the Cable and Wireless dinner he has complained of dodgy guts. Halfway through our warm-up at the ground, Jack sinks to his knees and goes green. All I can hear is 'shit, shit, shit...' He's cursing himself and his luck. He knows he's had it. Big blow for him as this would have been his 50th Test match and bad timing for Pat Murphy, BBC Radio reporter, who this morning has broadcast back home an interview with Jack about his new miracle diet which he expects will extend his career by several years.

Quick and drastic rethink. Stewart to keep wicket. Mark Butcher, who hasn't faced a ball all tour, nor since September come to that, is drafted in to bat at No.3. Alec will open if we bat first, but Butcher gets the nod ahead of Ramps on the basis that if Alec has to keep for a long period, Butch can open with Athers second time around. Butch is told half an hour before the start of play that he's in. Crawley drops down from no.3 to no.6.

That having been resolved, there is big build up of excitement in the dressing room. Forget the pre-tour training in Lanzarote, forget a week in the rain in Antigua, forget the farce at Jarrett Park, forget the flat one at Chedwin Park, THIS is what we are here for and it's coming now. Nerves doing cartwheels on the high wire. Adrenalin pumping.

Discuss in advance of the toss what to do if Athers wins it. Some think we should stick them in to try and draw first blood, but, bearing in mind the uncertainties over the pitch, the general feeling is that as it will only get worse we should take first crack, get out there and put a score on the board. One thing is certain: batting last is likely to be a nightmare.

Athers wins the toss. We will bat. The batsmen go through their own routines. Stewart opening his eyes as wide as he can to get adjusted to the light. Athers quietly composes himself.

The mood and atmosphere of quiet focus is slightly confused by a pre-match innovation which is pure showbiz. One by one, as we walk out onto the pitch for the national anthems, we are introduced individually to the crowd. Our press officer Brian Murgatroyd, with micro-phone in hand, gives it the full Madison-Square-Garden Monty: 'Graaaa-yeermm Thorrrpe, Phiiuuullip Tuffff-neell' etc, then we all line up one in front of one another facing downfield for *God Save the Queen* etc.

Quick glance around the ground to try and take it all in. Dean Headley is pumped up, standing there in front of a bloody great stand with his grandad's name written in three-foot-high letters at the back. He gets a big cheer when he comes out. To our left, looking out of our viewing platform on the dressing-room terrace, is the old Kingston Cricket Club pavilion, to which when he first came here, the legendary George would not have been admitted due to the colour of his skin.

Look across at the West Indies boys and notice that Lara is looking a trifle sheepish. A bit of booing when his name is read out, but a lot of applause as well and as they walk out on to field, Lara and Walsh conspicuously and rather clumsily shake hands as a public show of unity. In the far corner, under the scoreboard, bikini-clad Sandals girls are slipping into the tiny swimming pool, fruit punch in hand. You could be at Lord's.

Big, blue, cloudless hot sky. Come on. Come on. Good luck, Athers, Good luck, Al. Settle down in front of the dressing room telly. Game on.

Fifty-six minutes and 62 balls later. Game off. Blimey

First ball, no problem. Courtney, coming in from the far end from us, floats up a gentle loosener which Athers leans into and pushes away in front of square on the leg side for a single. Lovely, lovely, what's all the fuss about? Second ball, nothing much. Third ball pitches on a good length far enough outside off stump for Athers to shape to leave it in comfort, then jags right AT HIS HEAD. He manages to get inside it, just, and it sails past his left ear through to wicket-keeper David Williams. No real response inside the dressing-room. We've seen Courtney before and that kind of delivery before. More for something to do than anything else, Nasser leaves the viewing area and goes inside the dressing-room to fetch an arm guard from his coffin. Fourth ball lands in almost exactly the same spot, scuttles through never higher than 12 inches off the deck and bounces twice on its way through to Williams. A few eyes dart around the dressing-room to gauge reaction, but no major cause for alarm. Uneven bounce, but that can happen early on when the ball is hard and the pitch a little damp. No-one wants to do themselves in the brain before they actually go out to bat. Last two balls are pretty harmless. Gus announces he is going to have a kip.

Second over. Curtly to Alec from the George Headley Stand end. To the second ball of the over, Alec mis-times a drive off the front foot through mid-wicket for two runs. Fourth ball, he is hit high on the right arm by one that flies off a length. Lara takes the ball at first slip and leads half-hearted appeals for a catch. Umpire Venkat is unmoved. In the dressing-room Butch, next man in, exclaims: 'Jeesus Chrisst...' Play is suspended while Wayne Morton makes his first appearance to treat Stewie's shoulder. The speakers at the Sandals beach area blare out: 'The harder they come, the harder they fall.' Already Butch has noticed something rather peculiar. He points out: 'I've seen these guys before. This isn't quick. They're not bending their backs yet and Amby is bowling with no 'wheels' at all. But the ball is just hitting the deck and accelerating.'

Third over. Walsh to Athers. First up, Athers tries to shoulder arms to leave a ball outside off stump. It climbs vertically, smacks into the middle of his bat and straight to third slip where Sherwin Campbell, diving full stretch to his left, takes a belter. 4 for one. Err...

Good luck, Butch, all the best, mate. He walks out to join his brother-in-law (Butch is married to Judy, Alec's sister) and Alec's family greeting is: 'You wanted to be here.' Butch's first innings in competitive cricket for five months lasts precisely one delivery. The ball in question lifts violently from just short of a length and cuts him in two, ballooning off the bat handle. Stuart Williams takes the catch in the gully. Cheerio and thanks for coming. Later, after he has kicked a few things in the dressing room then calmed down, he describes the experience: 'I don't actually know what happened. Courtney looked like he was running in quick, but his arm came over with no sort of pace at all, no snap, nothing. I got into a great position and the next thing I knew the ball's taken the express elevator and is going straight to the top floor. I think it's going to clean me up (i.e. hit him on the nut), so I jerk my head out of the way and just feel the ball hit something, top of the handle, I think. I then look around to see if I can see where the ball has gone and it's looping straight to Williams in the gully. I just stood there for a few moments as much because of disorientaion as anything else. Afterwards, I sat in the dressing-room and went through the moment a hundred times wondering if there was any way I could have played the ball better. But then, after watching the television replay, I felt a lot better. As far as I am concerned, it was the first literally unplayable ball I have ever faced.'

Up in the Headley Stand, Ramps, who has taken up position here to watch, quietly asks himself: 'What the f*** is going on?' England are 4 for two.

I dive into my coffin to check that I have packed all my protective gear. Then I start to try on various arm guards in unusual positions, attempting to strap one across my shoulder blade. It is all going off. Fraser, woken up by the frenzied activity enquires: 'Anything happened yet?'. Alec welcomes Nass to the crease with the words: 'It's Saturday. It's eight o'clock. It's the lottery.' Nass nudges his fourth ball to fine leg for a single.

At the end of the over the umpires Venkat and Bucknor makes their first walkie-talkie call to match referee Jarman expressing concern over the state of the pitch.

Fourth over. Ambrose to Hussain. Nass plays out a maiden. The unease inside the dressing-room subsides slightly.

Not for long. Fifth over. Walsh to Stewart. Second ball: Alec fends off and manages to keep down a ball that flies off a good length. Third ball: Pitches in same spot but scuttles along the ground. Fourth ball: Pitches in same spot and darts past the outside edge of Alec's bat. Fifth ball: Pitches in same spot and cuts back viciously between bat and pad. Keeper Williams and Walsh half-heartedly appeal for a catch.

The umpires confer again with Jarman over the walkie-talkies.

Sixth over. Ambrose to Nasser. Fourth ball: Hussain is hit on the right index finger when the ball lifts off a fullish length. Morton makes his second appearance of the match and administers spray. We are quite worried as this is the finger Nass has broken twice before. At the end of the over Al and Nass confer and agree that they must try and play some shots. 'If we stay here prodding around, we'll get hit, or out and the innings will go nowhere,' Nass says. Alec agrees.

Seventh over. Walsh to Stewart. Second ball: Al takes two off his legs with a sketchy forcing shot. Fourth ball. Ditto. End of over score: England 9 for two.

Eighth over. Ambrose to Hussain. Second ball. Hussain pushes tentatively at a straight delivery and is caught by Carl Hooper at second slip. Make that 9 for three.

In the dressing-room, a kind of hysteria is taking hold. Butcher has come outside to sit next to Smokes, his county captain and his mate. Smokes, unsure of whether Butch wants to chat, stays silent. Butch looks at him out of the corner of his eye, Smokes looks back and when their eyes meet Smokes starts pissing himself with laughter.

It spreads. Thorpey is next man in and as he leaves the viewing area to replace Nasser, the man currently ranked the third best batter in world cricket is giggling like a schoolboy. He continues sniggering to himself all the way to the wicket. When he gets there, he makes a little comment to Al and they both burst out laughing.

Almost as soon as Nass has taken off his pads and gloves, Athers goes to him and asks: 'What's the form? Is the pitch as bad as it looks?' Nass says no, it's worse. Vice-captain informs captain that the surface is now crumbling and that no two deliveries are behaving alike. A plan is formulated – from now on we've all got to go out with all guns blazing. If we're going down, we're going down fighting. Smokes, due in after Crawley, is singled out as the man who must 'shoot from the hip'. He eagerly agrees and starts prowling around the dressing-room practising HUGE shots.

Ninth over. Walsh to Stewart. First ball Al cuts hard through the offside field. Shivnarine Chanderpaul saves the boundary, the batsmen run three. Fourth ball: Thorpe is hit on the left hand by a ball that rears up from a length. Morton makes his third appearance in 44 minutes. The speakers blare out 'Dangerous...' Thorpe's attention is attracted to the Sandals beach area, where some bloke hands his rum punch to a girl in a bikini then slips into the pool. He's intrigued by this chap's perspective on what is happening on the field. Umpires contact Jarman again, expressing serious concern, and by this time Athers has made his first visit to the back of Jarman's room, situated right next to our viewing area to make sure he is watching what we are watching.

By now I have retired to the relative safety of the dressing room and a group of us are following delivery by delivery on telly. Every ball is getting a reaction. Every ball is a potential grubber, hand or head breaker. This has stopped being a cricket match. Now it's just an exercise in not getting hit. Television camera zooms in on the landing area of one delivery from Courtney. In close-up you can see the ball pitch and fly upwards, carrying in its wake a piece of the pitch. They replay this over and over again, causing the boys to become a trifle animated. In the back of my mind, I am starting to think: hold on, I'm going to be batting out there in a moment. If this is what it's like in the ninth over, what's it going to be like in an hour's time, let alone four days? End of over score: England 12 for three.

Tenth over. Ambrose to Stewart. Second ball is a no-ball that flies off a good length and hits Al on the left hand. Thorpey calls for a run as the ball slides past second slip. Stewart has dropped the bat and shouts 'no'. Embers turns to Bumble and says: 'On reflection, I think I might possibly have taken the single.' Stewie beckons Morton to come on again.

Fourth ball. Perhaps the most extraordinary delivery of the match. It bursts through the surface just short of half-volley length, takes off and passes Al's outside edge and over the leaping Williams for four byes, very nearly six. At this the dressing-room has gone berserk. Creeps is shouting: 'This is f***ing ridiculous', Butch and Nass are flinging things around the room and Smokes is screaming: 'Come on. I'm going out there. Let me get out there.' Athers quietly slides around the back to see Jarman again. The West Indies fielders join Al at the spot where the ball pitches and they all just stand there staring at the hole in the pitch. Amby says to Al: 'There's nothing I can do about it.' Al is going a bit loopy at this stage, asking the umpires: 'What's the procedure? Is this fit for play? What's the procedure?'

Amby chuckles and walks back to his mark.

Last ball of over. Stewart is struck on the left hand for the second time in the over, his third blow of the match, and drops the bat again. Morton appears for the fifth time to administer running repairs. Stewart turns to Venkat and asks: 'Are we carrying on?'. Venkat and Bucknor confer at length with each other and Jarman. End of over score: England 17 for three.

Eleventh over. Walsh to Thorpe. First ball: Thorpey is hit on the arm by a ball that explodes from nowhere. Drops his bat. Morton makes his sixth appearance. The dressing room is in uproar. The speakers play: *Hit the Road Jack*. Someone says simply: 'For God's sake. This is crazy.'

The umpires call for the drinks cart to be brought out. On the telly the scene is like something from the Somme. The camera zooms in on Alec, who is sitting down rubbing his hand, then pans across to Thorpey who is on the deck having his arm sprayed by Wayne. Suddenly we see an unexpected and quite amazing sight. ATHERS IS ON THE PITCH.

Double-take. I look around the dressing-room to make sure I'm not imagining things. HE CAN'T BE OUT THERE. HE CAN'T BE ON THE PITCH. BUT HE IS. Up to this point, although we were all ranting and raving about the pitch, no-one actually believed any action would be taken. Now what?

Conversations are now taking place all over the pitch. Jarman is out there with Athers, Lara and the umpires all locked in discussions. The West Indies supporters in the George Headley Stand are shouting: 'Get on with it.'

The next thing we know, Athers, Alec and Thorpey are marching off the field. Where are they going? The umpires move slowly towards the dressing-rooms, Lara goes back to his team and starts talking to them in a huddle. Some of the press guys are wandering across the outfield from the press box at the other side of the ground. Nobody seems to know what the hell is happening, least of all us. Brian Murgatroyd is pacing up and down in his size fourteens. Athers has disappeared, so have the umpires, so has Jarman. Total and utter chaos.

Caddy has a bet with Chalks; $J100 that the game is going to be called off. Meanwhile Smokes is still marching around, shouting at himself.

As time goes by it is clear that something big is going down. Mniutes pass and there is no real news forthcoming. We all surmise this is because although the match is clearly not going to continue, nobody actually wants to be the one who says we should call it off. Then, after about half an hour or so, Bennett and Athers come into the dressing room and ask for quiet.

Bennett announces: 'The match has been called off.'

Total silence. Shock.

'The match has been abandoned, because the umpires consider the pitch unfit for play,' he continues, and then makes a statement that defies belief: 'Whatever you do, whatever you say, if anyone asks you about the pitch, tell them you cannot comment.'

Struggle to take this in. The match has been called off because the pitch is unfit for play ... but we cannot comment on the pitch. Not absolutely sure I get it. A few of the lads point out that as the state of the pitch is going to be the only topic of conversation for the next day or two, and the only thing the press men, quite rightly, are going to want to know is what we feel about it, this blanket ban on discussing it might be going a little too far. What is more, the moment one of us says we have been told not to say anything they will have field day.

After a few minutes of discussion, the management relents. The new message is this: Just don't go gobbing off too quick. Keep you heads down, get back to the pub and see what develops.'

The next piece of news raises more eyebrows and causes some disquiet. While the waiting and wondering was going on, talks were taking place between Athers, our management and their Board about what the hell they were going to do to get out of this mess.

Now we find out. It has been agreed that we will play an extra Test match to replace this one, starting in Trinidad next week.

Suddenly realise that this means we will be playing back-to-back Tests in Port-of-Spain and, bearing in mind the likely state of the pitch there, one or two of the lads, already pissed off over what has happened here, are not exactly thrilled. Their reasoning is this: Whoever is specifically responsible, this is the West Indies' cock-up. It's their fault that the pitch was not ready and is dangerous, yet they are asking us to squeeze in another Test match to save face for them, another Test at short notice for which we will have no real proper preparation, at the Queen's Park Oval ground where not only we were bowled out for 46 last time round in 1994, but which last week was condemned for producing a pitch unfit for first-class cricket. It is going to be hard enough to do well out here anyway, but why should we be penalised for their incompetence?

All such arguments are given very short shrift. Athers says we have come to play a five-Test series and that is what we are going to do. We're going to play back-to-back Tests in Trinidad and that's that. No arguments, no further discussions. So make the best of it.

The riot police have arrived with their helmets and guns. We are told to stay inside the dressing-room just in case things turn nasty. Athers and Bumble go off to face the media and we get ready to leave. A couple of hours after everyone walked off the pitch, we get on the bus to go back to the hotel.

Very strange feeling on leaving the ground. Some of the England supporters are still wandering around, looking completely bewildered. For some of these this trip was the holiday of a lifetime. Some have saved for a long time, and maybe for some retired people this is the first chance they've had. They've travelled to Jamaica to watch the first Test between England and West Indies and after just 62 balls, they'll have to travel home with nothing but disappointment to show for it. Some of them will never have the chance again. Somehow, in the back of your mind, you feel a bit responsible.

It's too early to make any real analysis or assessment of what went wrong. The only feeling we have is that, like the supporters, we have been cheated out of a Test match. This is what we have prepared for, this is what we have set our minds to and focused on, and at 2 o'clock on the first day we are back at the hotel twiddling our thumbs and saying sorry to an awful lot of upset people.

Decide to try and get away from what has happened. Fix up dinner with co-author and Lisa and Claire at Strawberry Hill restaurant up in the hills. During the 45-minute journey, lots of gallows humour about the match until our driver, very politely, asks us to stop. He is ashamed, he says. This is a disaster and will be seen by outsiders as clear evidence that Jamaicans cannot be trusted to organise anything, let alone a Test match. At one stage he has to stop the van as he is close to tears. Suddenly, you realise the effect on the local people of what has happened.

Strawberry Hill is amazing, with a quite unbelievable view of the lights of Kingston spread out beneath us, and spirits are raised by a good meal and a fair amount of very delicious wine. Near the end of the meal, a bloke whose face rings a bell comes toward our table. No-one is really in the mood to field another set of questions about what went wrong, but, as it happens, this guy doesn't want to know anyway. His name is Robbie Williams.

Lisa nearly faints, as does Claire. Turns out he's a cricket nut and, what's more, he says he's always wanted to meet me! Do not laugh. Huge cred with Lisa.

Nice bloke. Prone to exclaiming 'Fantastic' rather a lot, but very polite, almost deferential in the presence of a megastar like me, and after a brief chat he slips away quietly. He's staying at Strawberry Hill and he's off to his room to watch the match between Jamaica and Sweden on the box. Can't quite get used to the idea of Robbie Williams holed up in a hotel room watching football on the telly. Is this what the Stones did in their heyday?

Accept co-author's offer of a glass of port which, unbeknown to him at this stage, is about to set him back £60. (No wonder he went a strange colour when the bill arrived.) We repair to the beautiful lounge lit up by an open log fire and full of ornate furniture and romantically inclined couples getting in some serious moonlit chat. Just to complete the picture, I lean back on my wrought-iron chair, keep going, fail to right myself and fall crashing to earth in a heap. The chair legs have skidded under me, cutting deep trenches in the polished wooden floor. Completely flummoxed, I rise to my feet, almost shouting my apologies to all present: 'I AM TERRIBLY SORRY. I AM TERRIBLY SORRY.' A lady I have never seen in my life before leans over and, in a rather resigned tone of voice, says: 'Oh, it's you, Philip.'

Zebedee says, 'Time for bed.'

CHAPTER FIVE

The Aftermath

Friday 30 January

The aftermath. This morning's copy of *The Gleaner* makes desperate reading. A reporter named Tym Glaser, the Associate Editor (Sport), has rounded up a batch of reactions from travelling Brits. If we felt bad enough waking up to find yesterday was not some sort of mass hallucination, reading this little lot makes us all feel ten times worse.

Peter Hill, a 62-year-old flooring contractor from Birmingham: 'It's the first time I have been to the West Indies and I won't be coming back. We spent four days on the north coast in Port Antonio expecting to fish for Blue Marlin and we couldn't hire a boat. We thought the Test would be the salvation of the trip, but now we are absolutely devastated.'

Jeff Stammers, a 31-year-old computer specialist from Kenilworth: 'When we get back, everybody will be laughing at us. We sat down and went through the five Tests and chose this one as the best to attend. Now we are absolutely gutted. It is really upsetting and has wasted our holidays.'

About the only fans interviewed who didn't seem too worried were a band of Scots wearing T-shirts proclaiming them as the 'Jamaican Lubrication Delegation from the Scottish nation'.

As for the unravelling of what actually went on in those last few minutes of the match, the full story is emerging bit by bit. After Thorpey had been hit by that last ball, Athers had actually been beckoned onto the field by Alec. Then Athers and the umpires discussed what had been happening and they asked him for his opinion. He then conferred with Lara and asked him if he agreed that the conditions were dangerous and unfit for play. Lara agreed, the two captains communicated their thoughts to the umpires and to Jarman, and then everyone left the field.

In the immediate period after the abandonment everyone had their say. Richie Richardson, the former Windies captain, said he thought we should have carried on. Michael Holding, their former great fast bowler and a proud Jamaican, said: 'I've never seen a pitch as dangerous as that. It wasn't fit for Test cricket or even club cricket, for that matter. It was completely sub-standard, Our fast bowlers don't want to seriously injure anyone. It was an embarrassment.'

Jarman: 'It was horrid. It was nowhere near standard. Someone would definitely have been badly hurt if play had continued.'

Bucknor: 'I've never before officiated in a Test match when I've been worried the batsman could be hit every ball. Each time I was thinking "This could be the one." What concerned me was the unprotected area below the ear and at the side and back of the head. Also a powerful blow to the heart or ribs could have been dangerous'.

Athers: 'Both sides and the match officials were in agreement. The pitch was dangerous and the safety of the players must always be paramount. It was unfit for first-class cricket.'

Morton: 'It was war out there. Altogether Alec got hit five

times – on the forearm twice, both hands and the shoulder.'

Alec: 'You knew you were going to take hits. It was just a case of when and how many. If it had gone on much longer, I'd have ended up looking like that lady who's just appeared before a French court.'

Nasser: 'It was like standing up against a firing squad and trying to dodge the bullets.'

Even today the reaction among the players is still one of shock. I've never experienced anything like it, and more and more I'm feeling as though I've been robbed of something precious. We all feel upset for the supporters, but deep down I feel bitter that a Test match I should have been involved in has just been nicked and thrown away.

The thing people must remember is that this was supposed to be a five-day Test match on a pitch that is meant to last for five days. If the pitch had deteriorated naturally and behaved like that on the final day, then you might have thought that was fair enough. Alec and Athers and the other guys have faced Curtly and Courtney on wickets that were doing a bit, and they have taken the odd blow on the gloves, on the arm or shoulder, even the nut. But this was different. This was out of control. There was no skill involved, no judgement of the ball to leave alone etc. This was a matter of either getting hit or not depending on pure luck – the game of Test cricket reduced to a lottery – and these things were happening not at the end of a match but during the first hour of the first morning. If people are allowed to get away with preparing terrible wickets like this one, then Test matches are going to be over and done in two days and the game is going to be dead.

As for the squeezing in of an extra Test, a lot of the boys believe this to be belittling the status of Test cricket. It's almost like being on a club tour. We came out here to play a five-Test series and now they're saying let's bung another one in. I feel for the supporters, but most of the people who missed out in Jamaica will be long gone back to England before this extra match starts next week. By rights we should carry on with the rest of the itinerary as scheduled, but, as always, we have to be seen to be doing the right thing: bending over backwards to accommodate everyone else even if it means putting more pressure on ourselves. I cannot believe, for instance, that, faced with the same circumstances, the Australians would have agreed to do the same.

Some of the lads are talking about darker aspects, about the possibility that the West Indies authorities actually intended to make a pitch to suit their fast bowlers and that things just got out of hand. Who knows? There might even be something in this conspiracy theory, but I really do believe that the problem was incompetence rather than malice aforethought.

Interesting information comes from the groundsman Charlie Joseph, who has spent 30 years at Sabina Park. Charlie is renowned for making to order some of the fastest, but also flatest and truest pitches in the Caribbean. But it appears that this time, the preparation of the strip for the Test match was taken out of his hands.

Charlie had been aware for some time that the square where the pitches were, was near the end of its natural life. But the whole process was taken away from Charlie and sub-contracted to an outside firm and, by all accounts, they simply did not give themselves enough time. Apparently they travelled into the interior of Jamaica to find the right sort of clay, brought it back, plonked it down and expected a pitch to be made from it just like that.

When Charlie came back from a three-week holiday and saw the re-laid pitch, he realised something was wrong and told the authorities: 'The pitch does not have any compaction.'

Should he not have pressed the point? 'I have to follow what I am told to do. They are bigger people. You have to follow instructions. Myself, I know I could have done it better than this.'

Somewhat alarming development later in the day when the television news bulletins broadcast an interview with Lara that took place just after the match had been called off, in which he appears to be suggesting that we should have carried on. This is pissing off Athers big time. The press boys have got hold of Lara's quotes. 'We would most definitely have batted on,' he allegedly said.

'If the West Indies had batted first we would have seen it as the sort of situation where you have to fight it out as cricketers.

'It was dangerous, but a lot of our guys said if we were batting, it would have been tough to call off the game because we've experienced pitches such as this before. So the match might still be going on if we'd batted, but it was the umpires who made the final decision.'

Athers gets his chance to confront Lara when we all pitch up at a function thrown by the Jamaican Prime Minister for the players of both teams and the English supporters who have come all this way for nowt. Athers tracks Lara down and asks him what the hell is going on. Lara tells Athers that he had to say something to get the local media off his back. The bloke is under intense pressure here. A lot of the locals are convinced that we got the match called off, when we didn't, but Lara cannot be seen to be too acquiescent in all this. Athers accepts his explanation and the matter is resolved.

Oh, sod it. Lisa's gone home and we're leaving tomorrow. I can't be doing with any more of this.

Saturday 31 January. Kingston to Port-of-Spain, Trinidad

Cheered up no end by an hilarious piece by Geoff Boycott in *The Sun*. It was faxed over to us this morning and is a scream. First of all, he says that the Test match was called off too early.

'After 10 overs? Crikey, there needed to be three blokes in hospital for that to happen', he says.

So we should have waited until someone got killed before the match was abandoned, I presume.

'There were only two killer balls – the one that struck Alec Stewart on the shoulder and the one that dismissed Mark Butcher.' Just the two, then.

But he saved the best bits for last.

'I was able to steel my mind – that's why I played well on poor pitches.

'Probably the worst pitch I played on was at Abbeydale Park, Sheffield, for Yorkshire against Derbyshire in 1983. I carried my bat for an unbeaten century in the fourth innings.

'Ronnie Burnett, Yorkshire's chairman at the time, and Ray Illingworth, our manager, both said it was the finest innings they'd ever seen on a bad pitch. The ball was leaping and jumping all over the place.'

I'm sure it was Geoffrey, especially as the fearsome attack Boycs faced that day comprised Ole Mortensen, loony Danish paceman just starting in the game; Colin Tunicliffe, loopy medium slow; Dallas Moir, left-arm spin; and Geoff Miller, gentle rarely-turning off-breaks. A slightly different proposition to Curtly and Courtney, with 600 Test wickets between them.

'Bad pitches have always existed. Unless you can conquer fear you've got no chance.

'To me it was a challenge. I used to love it. I'd rather get hit than get out. Others were more worried about being carried off on a stretcher. I used to relish batting more on a tough track than a shirtfront. I used to think: 'This is a contest and no bugger's gonna get me out.'

One man most interested in Boycott's views was Ian Botham, who wondered whether Boycs might have been suffering from a bout of temporary amnesia when writing the piece. 'On the 1979-80 tour of Australia," recalls Beefy, "Boycott took one look at a dodgy pitch in Sydney on which we were due to play the second Test then another at an Aussie attack that included Dennis Lillee and Len Pascoe and shortly before play was due to start complained to Mike Brearley, the captain, that he had a sore neck and couldn't play. Brears knew exactly what Boycs was up to. He sent him into the nets then told him he had to play. Boycott scored eighteen and four and they won easily. Perhaps this was one occasion when he preferred to get out rather than hit."

One or two of the lads used to go to Boycs regularly for advice on batting, but the sad fact is that pieces like this undermine his credibility with the team. People who know say he was a fine player and quite shrewd when it came down to it, but this sort of thing is just cheap crap.

Leave Jamaica for Trinidad and a welcome change of scenery. Long flight, round the houses with a couple of stops. Collected by two prison buses with the words: 'Property of Trinidad Penitentiary' written on the sides. Slightly alarmed and a little bit shocked to find we are travelling with four armed soldiers in each bus, all toting machine guns. Hope this isn't a sign of the reaction to the first Test being called off.

Crawl into hotel late. Major kip.

CHAPTER SIX

The six lives of David Williams

Sunday 1 February

At last the latest issue of *The Thrutcher* arrives. It tells THAT Crofty/Creeps/sea urchin story in full:

'Croft in Crustacean Chaos: Robert Croft was entangled with a rather nasty opponent during the 18–30s trip to Sandals, Montego Bay. Squeezing into the water chute at the Margeuritteville Bar, the weighty Welshman made slow but jerky progress to the end of the chute, having been passed several times by slimmer players, before being spewed out into the pool. The splash caused a tidal wave and local insurance companies have been inundated with claims.

'The talkative taff was attempting to climb out of the pool when he stood on a sea urchin. At this point John "Creepy" Crawley, the Lancastrian graduate, jumped to his rescue with a home made remedy, namely whipping out his todger and p***ing all over the Welshman's foot.

Croft suffered stinging sensations to the foot and spent several hours having the offending spikes removed and the urine-affected areas disinfected. News of the mollusc is not good. It died on the poolside having had every ounce of breath expelled from its body by the whopping Welshman.'

* * *

I have been excused duty for the two-day practice match against Trinidad and Tobago at Guaracara Park which has been rearranged from a three-day contest because of the new scheduling. As the ground is situated right next to an oil refinery, with signs all over the place reading 'no naked flames' and 'no smoking', I reckon the reason I'm not playing is that they think I'd better not go in case I blow the place up. Instead, me and the other chaps not required go down to the Queen's Park Oval for nets. We get our first look at the Test pitch. Obviously, bearing in mind what happened at Sabina Park and the fact that the last first-class match here ended in two days, there is big interest in the surface and it looks nice and flat, if, as expected and predicted by Lara, a bit grassy. The point is emphasised by the selection of Kenny Benjamin in the West Indies squad. He hasn't played for them since he came home early from their 1996 tour of Australia, but he took eight in the match for Leewards against Trinidad and is the nearest they have to a specialist swing bowler.

The groundsman, Curtis Roberts and the ground co-ordinator Bryan Davis, former West Indies opener, insist there will be no worries over this pitch. I resolve to call Davis 'Mandy Rice' from now on. But apart from the greenness, the main concern is that he has had to prepare two pitches side by side because Sky television's camera positions dictate that the Test matches be played in the same area of the square. Natural wear and tear is one thing, but if you have bowlers running across from one strip across to the other in their follow through, the damage could be significant.

We can't actually practise on the square because there is a big game going on involving the local police team. Naturally.

Back at the hotel we wait for the boys to return from the

oil fields and when they do, coughing and spluttering and complaining of headaches, they say the fumes are terrible. It's a nothing match in terms of competitive cricket, but useful up to a point for match practice. We score 351 in the day but the batsmen are im-pressed by a young leg-spinner called Dinanath Ramnarine, who bowled 30 overs and took five for 72, getting out Athers, Alec, Chalks and Smokes – both for ducks – and Dean Headley. Can't imagine the Windies will play a specialist spinner in the series, but he is one for the notebook, as they say.

Phone home to make sure Lisa's back and okay and then, at last, the moment for which I have been waiting is here. Next on HBO … *The Best Of Autopsy*.

What can I say? Perfect in every respect and more than living up to its advance billing. The first case is a classic of its kind. The Corpse and the Jellyfish. Here's the story: the partially decomposed torso of an unknown woman has been discovered. To find out whodunit the police must first discover who she is. Could the two jellyfish found clinging to her chest be vital clues? Yes, they could. Why? You've guessed it … because they are not jellyfish, but silicone breast implants, both bearing a serial number from which she is later identified. You couldn't make it up. I ask you: first-class entertainment, or what? They should have this stuff on the Royal Variety Show.

Monday 2 February

This hotel, the Trinidad Hilton, is just brilliant. Built into the side of a cliff by some wacky 50s architect, almost certainly wearing a beatnik beard and out of his brains on mind-expanding drugs, it resembles the set of Tracy Island from *Thunderbirds*. The lobby is on the top deck and all the other floors are numbered in reverse order. If you want to go to the ninth floor, for instance, you either walk or take the lift *down* nine floors. This causes big confusion when you are on the ninth and want to go to the sixth – is that up or down?

The main bar is sunk three feet below the level of the floor, so that when you order a drink you have to stoop down and talk downwards. It's a bit like how I guess it would be to peer over the Chair at Aintree, and after you've had a few, about as dangerous. Sounds like recipe for a Derek Pringle type, pulled-a-muscle-writing-a-letter, injury. Imagine falling over and breaking a leg walking *into* a bar. With my reputation?

The swimming pool at the centre of the complex is a peculiar shape, sort of like a very thick lightning bolt, and if you let your mind wander you can half hear Jeff from *Thunderbirds* booming out: 'FIVE... FOURRR... THREEEE... TWOOOO... WUN' while the pool and its contents slide back to allow Scott and Thunderbird 1 to be launched skywards to save Alan's rocketship from crashing into the sun. What is in this fruit punch?

Most of the rooms have been refurbished since last time, which is a relief as the main feature of the decor then was that everything in the hotel was the colour brown, in all its shades.

Outside the main reception is swarm of tank-sized taxis. Trinidad being an island whose main natural resource is oil, the cabs are those huge barge-size American gas-guzzlers, all about a mile and a half from nose to tip and all palatially luxurious inside. Driving one of them must be like piloting a sofa.

The restaurant where we have breakfast is stunning. A massively high room with a winding staircase as its central feature and glass for walls. Minute and American attention to detail including a small card explaining in Spanish and English why you can only smoke in designated areas.

Entitled 'The Courtesy Of Choice' and with the yin segment of the yin/yang symbol (or is it the yang?) decorated with a lit cigarette, it reads: 'The concept and symbol of *The Courtesy Of Choice* reflect the centuries old philosophy that acknowledges differences while allowing them to exist together in harmony.

'*The Courtesy Of Choice* accommodates the preferences of individuals by offering both smoking and non-smoking areas in the spirit of conviviality and mutual respect.'

I only wanted a fag.

More largely futile attempts at nets and then the coughers and splutterers return from Guaracara Park. The Test match starts on Thursday and the boys are beginning to get geared up again now.

Tuesday 3 February

On the way down to the Queen's Park Oval for nets, we pass the Calypsonians and steel bands warming up for their part in Carnival. Don't get me wrong, the music is excellent, but I'm not particularly looking forward to trying to concentrate with that racket in my ear all the time.

David Rudder seems to be the king, although the official contest is a few days away yet and there is Krosfyah (as in Crossfire) and others to beat. On various Caribbean grounds over the two tours I've been on, I've listened to Rudder's great song *Rally Round the West Indies* a thousand times and never tire of hearing it again. His latest hit, *High Mas* is top drawer. It has caused a few problems with the local religious leaders as it starts with a line from the Lord's Prayer then continues with praises to Jah, but will be one of the highest profile tunes of the Carnival, which some of the holy believe is just one big baccanalian orgy. One Roman Catholic priest believes Rudder is being 'grossly sacrilegious'. Don't know about all that, but it's a catchy little number. Slightly less melodious but big fun is *Who let the dogs out?* I have absolutely no idea whatsoever what this song is all about, but the highlight comes when, at regular intervals, the singer shouts 'Who let the dogs out?' then he and his mates bark: 'WOOF! WOOF! WOOF! WOOF!' Move over Sir Tim Rice.

Wednesday 4 February

Thoughts focus on tomorrow's match. The pitch will be green, so the thinking is to keep the same XI that would have played at Sabina Park had Jack not been ill, namely: Atherton, Stewart, Crawley, Hussain, Thorpe, Hollioake, Russell, Caddick, Headley, Fraser, Tufnell. Butch, after facing one ball in Jamaica, is out. Hope that's not his tour.

Not quite sure how Ramps is taking all this, either. He passionately wants to get into his Test career again and feels right to push on and get some momentum going after making his runs at The Oval. Not making the first Test was bad enough for him, but, having not been selected for the truncated practice match at Guaracara Park, and now two Tests coming up back-to-back, his first chance of a proper bat will not come until the first-class match against Guyana *after* the third Test has been played here, some seven weeks into the tour. The lack of decent practice facilities here is really frustrating for him and he appears to be trying to get rid of his angst in the gym.

Talking of which, incidentally, the other fixture there is Adam Hollioake. Time after time I have been on my way down to the bar here and bumped into him in his shorts either coming back from or going to the gym. Fanatically, fantastically fit. Come to know him more as the trip has gone on. Extremely confident as well as physically strong and completely fearless. His dressing-room war cries at Sabina Park were no act. Have come to discover that this is the man to have alongside you if ever a night out starts to turn queer. First sign of trouble, call for Smokes. When he starts grunting like an ape and giving it the South Sea Island face-dancing, look out.

But there is brain behind the brawn as well. Big thinker about the game and his driving truth, it seems to me, is that there is absolutely no room in anyone's life for the slightest negative thought. Impressive.

Tomorrow, after the false start, the series actually begins. The mood is upbeat, the flag is down and all that. The message is that we must announce ourselves and impose ourselves and not be intimidated by anyone. This may be Lara's island, but none of us are going to allow him to dominate us or the proceedings. Just make sure everyone knows you're here.

Thursday 5 February, Second Test, Queen's Park Oval, Day 1

Close of play: England 1st inns 175–8 (Hussain 44*, Fraser 2*)
The back page of local paper *Newsday* is almost completely covered with a single photograph of one of the groundstaff mowing the pitch, with various officials in the background scratching their chins. The headline reads: 'WE READY FOR DEM' in huge letters. Jolly good.

Unfortunately, they are not quite. There has been a problem with the sightscreen at the pavilion end of the ground for some time. Last year, the authorities put up a canvas sheet and the members promptly hacked it down because it obscured their view. Something is in place this time and the members have been asked to leave it alone but, at the other end, they are still draping a tarpaulin up against one side of the media centre as the umpires walk onto the field.

For the first time on this tour, we are aware of the presence of the Barmy Army here. With the odd exception they are good people and you can't buy their enthusiasm. There were problems in Perth during the Test match there on the last Ashes tour, when some of the locals wanted to have a bit of a go and a rumpus ensued, but by and large their support is welcome.

They will have their work cut out here to match the locals, the Trini Posse, mad keen Lara supporters who sing and dance to *High Mas, Toro, Toro* and *Who let the dogs out?* fuelled by large quantities of rum.

Game on. Athers wins the toss again and we are to bat first, basically for the same reasons as we did at Sabina Park. The pitch looks much better than that, but the feeling is that there will be uneven bounce and that it will only get worse as the match goes on.

It's hard work, with all the batters having to wear a few. Amby and Walsh enjoy themselves again early on and although Alec bats like God, we are soon up against it. The ball is moving off the seam a lot and coming through at different heights, and the boys are getting hit on the gloves regularly. For the first time we notice the effect of the high seam balls we are using for this series. They are a lot like the ones outlawed towards the end of the 1980s in England after ordinary medium pacers managed to make the ball dance and sing. The larger seam grips the surface and makes the ball jag about violently, especially if the pitch is green or slightly moist.

Alec's 50 gets us out of the embarrassment zone, but at

tea we are only 114 for four, with Athers, Alec, Creeps and Chalks all gone. Shortly afterwards, things go from bad to worse when Smokes is given run out in controversial circumstances.

We've had it drummed into us, quite rightly, that we must be on the lookout for quick singles, both to keep the scoreboard moving and avoid getting stuck. Traditionally, it has always been very difficult to score quickly against Ambrose and Walsh. They are not only brilliant at getting people out when the pitches offer the slightest assistance, but they are also bloody miserly when it comes to balls you can hit. If they find nothing is doing for them they will slow everything down, post fielders in a widish circle to cut off the runs, and just sit tight and wait. Then, when they take one wicket they pile in, and it is ALL ON – bouncers, yorkers, throat balls, banzai … and very often collapses follow (don't mention the 46).

Thanks to all the hard work we have been put through by Bumble and his team our boys are lightning between wickets, but there are bound to be mistakes when you are pushing for singles. This time, Nass, who is batting well and confidently, drives a ball firmly and calls for the run without realising that the ball is going too close to Shivnarine Chanderpaul in the covers. Smokes responds to the call, but Chanderpaul fields the ball cleanly and throws it towards keeper David Williams in one movement. Halfway down the track, Smokes gets that horrible feeling that he is not going to make it. But then both he and Nass, who has made his ground at the bowler's end and has turned to watch, then notice that, in the process of collecting the ball, Williams has inadvertently knocked off one of the bails before then hitting the stumps to complete the run out.

Venkat, the umpire square of the wicket, has Williams's back between him and the stumps so he cannot see the whole picture, but knowing that Smokes is well out of his ground and assuming no complications, he raises the finger and gives Smokes out.

At this, Nass has a quiet word with Steve Bucknor, the umpire at the bowler's end, to tell him what he has seen. On the way back to the hutch Smokes also pauses to tell Venkat: 'I think the bail was dislodged.'

By this time we're all crowded around the television in the dressing-room to see what is going on. Venkat signals the sign of the box to the third umpire up at the top of the media centre, Clyde Cumberbatch. Smokes and Nass are so sure that the television replays will lead to a reprieve that they meet in the middle to discuss plans for the rest of the partnership, including taking a bit more care over the quick runs. But Cumberbatch takes one look at the replay from the view that Venkat has seen, and because he thinks he is only supposed to be confirming whether the batsman was out of his ground, quickly signals that he is out.

Smokes is genuinely taken aback.

Even before he has returned to the pavilion, we see why. The Sky producer has replayed the incident from front-on, Nasser's end, and zoomed in on the keeper's gloves and the stumps. From this it could quite clearly be seen that Williams had, in fact, knocked off the bail by accident, before taking the throw from Chanderpaul.

Then comes the next stage of discussion. Even though the bail had been dislodged before Williams performed the run out, did his subsequent hitting of the stump with the ball in his glove constitute a clean run out? The answer, according to the Laws of Cricket, is no.

The rules state that if a bail has been dislodged, the

wicket-keeper or fielder must then remove the remaining bail, or uproot a stump to complete the run out, neither of which Williams did.

In other words, it's a cock-up. Smokes is quite calm about it when he gets back. He just shrugs his shoulders and says 'it was a shit run, anyway.' But the incident does highlight weaknesses in a system that is designed to help avoid wrong decisions being made. The technology exists, it seems, to make these matters watertight. But if you don't employ it, it's about as much use as a chocolate teapot.

After all the excitement has died down, the realisation hits that we are deep in the crapper and when Jack goes next over, second ball to young Nixon McLean, we are 126 for six on what is, in effect, the first full day of the series.

When Caddy goes in to replace Jack I look around the dressing-room and see Deano and Gus getting themselves quietly ready. Then I suddenly realise I'm IN AFTER THEM. Oh, Christ! Pads, pads, where's my pads? Gloves, box, get the box, arm guards, everything.

It is difficult to describe the panic that ensues when you realise you could be batting in two deliveries' time and you aren't ready. There is a recurring nightmare suffered regularly by some batsmen that goes like this: A wicket falls and they are next man in and they realise they don't have a stitch on. Then, when they try to get ready, it takes absolutely hours. No matter how hard they try to get a move on, they just don't seem to get anywhere. The dream either ends when they wake up or when they finally get out to the middle to find someone has got there before them and taken their place in the batting order. I'm feeling a bit like that now. Or is that just wishful thinking?

Fortunately, Nass is batting really well. He's been hit a number of times as Curtly and Courtney are making it go one way, then the other. He's taken one on the arm that will leave a colourful badge in the morning.

The other lads do a brilliant job to support Nass. Caddy manages to hang around, taking a couple of hits into the bargain and after him, in the face of a real barrage, Deano also stands tall. That is until one bumper too many rears up and hits him smack on the side of the head. The clanging sound is clearly audible back in the dressing-room. The impact of the blow literally knocks him off his feet, and his senses are so scrambled that his attempts to get back into his crease resemble the Saturday night shuffle. Nass gets down the other end to check he is okay, and Deano tells him that although he knew he had to get back he didn't know which way back was. He removes his helmet and a dirty great hard boiled egg has already started to sprout.

Deano carries on but his bravery counts for little when he is soon out in the second set of controversial circum-stances of the day. Amby, getting a bit pissed off that the tail-end charlies are hanging around, decides to bowl round the wicket at Deano's body. A fair enough ploy in itself and usually very effective. But in order to get the best possible angle for the deliveries, he is bowling from *very* wide of the crease. On more than one occasion the Sky cameras show that he is bowling from so wide that he is actually cutting the return crease, and as such should be called by the umpire Steve Bucknor for no-balling. Unfortunately, the ball which gets Deano caught at the wicket is one of these.

In the dressing room the guys are feeling that the luck is not really going for us today.

After Deano, Gus comes in and defies logic, form and history by surviving the chin music against against two of the very best in the business, and surviving until the close, when we are 175 for eight, with Nass not out on 44.

Not great, but not as bad as it could have been, and on this pitch, who knows?

Knackered from watching all this, so early to bed. Before I nod off, I go through what is likely to happen tomorrow. Just spend a cheeky half-hour imagining what it is going to be like and how I am going to deal with it. End up dreaming of many fine shots, pulling Curtly for four over mid-wicket and walking down the track to hit Courtney over extra-cover. Bit like that dream you have the night before you have to go to the dentist, when everything has gone fine and you're back at home laughing about how daft it was to be worried in the first place. Then you wake up...

Friday 6 February, Second Test, Day 2

England 1st inns 214 all out; West Indies 1st inns 177–7 (Ambrose 20*, Benjamin 0*)

And then I wake up...

And so does Gus when, first thing, he gets crusted by Kenny Benjamin. In all, he takes six blows and if he stops punching them the bruises will be gone by early April. The waiting to go to the wicket is awful. I'm not scared exactly, although being able to withstand physical pain has never been one of my more obvious qualities, it's just that I'm desperate not to let anyone down.

Gus helps Nass drag us past 200 and onward, making a fantastic 17 out of their ninth wicket stand of 42, which is about half the number of fags I consume while sitting there, waiting for my turn, decked out with at least one item of every form of protective equipment known to man. I look like the Michelin Man.

Then, finally, the moment the West Indies bowlers have been longing for arrives. Gus is unlucky to be given out caught behind, off his sleeve if anything, then I rise from the chair, splash through the pool of sweat that has formed underneath it and head out towards my moment of destiny. Sensing my quite palpable unease, Ramps offers a few words of encouragement: 'Get in line. You can hang around a bit. Look at what Gus has done.' Without thinking, I say to myself: 'Yeah. Why f***ing not?', then suddenly realise he is talking about me. Me. Philip Tufnell. Get in line and hang around a bit against the most fearsome pair of fast bowlers in world cricket? With my reputation? As I pass Gus, I congratulate him briefly then ask the question he has heard me ask a thousand times before.

'Is it quick?'

Gus smiles. 'A little bit,' he says.

Right. I'm here now. Come on, come on, you bastards. I'm not afraid of you. I take guard, try to ignore the sniggering from the close-in fielders and wait for my first ball from Benjamin. Now, watch the ball … get in line, get in line, stay in line, get behind it, watch it, watch it … sod it.

Thick edge. Caught Lara. First ball.

Very disappointing. Get back to the dressing-room and unstrap all the armour, feeling a bit silly. Just goes to show I shouldn't have wasted my time thinking about it the night before. All that build-up and I survive one ball and now I'm facing a king pair against the West Indies on a green seaming wicket. Not a great thought to be carrying around.

Still, we've made 214 which could be anything. Don't know how the wicket is going to play from here on in, but we have a score on the board and from 126 for six, a massive one.

And the rest of the day belongs to us and, more specifically, to Gus. Deano makes an early breakthrough, having Sherwin Campbell caught by Jack at 16 for one. Lara appears to a huge reception on his first Test as captain in his native Trinidad and starts as though he has a plane to catch. For us, the game goes a bit dead, until Gus is given his first bowl.

Like 'genius', 'lumbering' is a word often misused. But in Gus's case, how else can you describe what he looks like when he starts his painfully-long looking run to the wicket. 'I'M NOT TIRED. I'M NOT TIRED' are the words running round my brain as he begins again. But when he finally gets there, a whirl of arms (no classic delivery action this) and the ball, more often than not, comes out arrow-straight. Gus admits he never tries to do much with the ball, just lands it in the right place and hopes it will hit the seam and go one way or the other. Even on a flat one the batsmen know they cannot take any chances, but here on this pitch, with this high-seamed ball, Gus makes shot-making almost suicidally risky.

Here he comes, chugging in like Thomas the Tank Engine's grumpy mate, Angus, the give-us-twenty-five-overs-uphill-and-into-the-wind engine. But this time when the balls bounce, they jag. Williams is caught by Athers: 42 for two. Hooper goes too far across his sticks and is bowled around his legs: 48 for three. In the game … we are back in the game.

But still something in the back of everyone's mind says don't push it with the big man. He will willingly bowl all day and all night, as he did against Lara in Antigua four years ago, but realistically in this heat, five or six-over spells are all you can expect of anyone, let alone a 32-year-old.

So Caddy is given another crack while Gus takes a breather, and then all hell breaks loose. Caddy has been quoted in the local papers and back home as saying that he has a plan to get Lara out. Everyone has made a big thing of this and, in hindsight, it might have been slightly wiser for him to say such things after the event rather than before.

Whether Lara read the comments or cares in the slightest, no-one knows, but he launches into the bloke with seemingly vicious intent, and with Chanderpaul, takes 27 off three of his overs immediately after tea, smacking him to all parts and out of the attack.

I am summoned to accompany Gus and the message is give them nothing. Bowling from the media centre end, I find it hard to get my length and rhythm right. When I bowl over the wicket to the left-handers into the rough, I tie them up but, instead of playing me with the bat they just kick me away. In county cricket, if the blokes start doing this too much I know the umpires will give me a couple of lbws and then the batsmen are forced to play, but here in Test cricket things are somewhat different. I have to settle for trying to keep the lid on. Duty calls.

In any case, it starts to work as the frustration me and Gus are putting on their batters gets under their skin. Gus snares Chanderpaul, edging a drive to Chalks at slip and then, minutes later, Lara is bored out. He tries to clip one from Gus through mid-on and mistimes the shot straight to Athers at mid-off.

This wicket brings an extraordinary response from Gus. Okay, it *is* Lara in the back pocket and all that, but Gus is positively exploding with delight. As we are in the huddle, Athers, who has noticed this rare display of exuberance says, jokingly: 'Calm down, it's only Lara.' Gus responds: 'Lara? Sod Lara. That's my 123rd Test wicket, one more than Ray Illingworth.'

Gus and Raymond never did see eye to eye. Illy had started to identify Gus as ripe for the chop during our last visit here and, within a season of becoming chairman of selectors in April 1994, had employed all his vast cricketing knowledge to boot him out of the reckoning for the winter tour to Australia, against Athers' wishes and better judgement. Not that anyone in the Middlesex dressing-room has ever heard Gus utter anything but the highest praise for Raymond, of course, but this wicket gives Fraze something tangible over Illy at last – namely more Test wickets.

Now we understand. And now we're cooking. Jimmy Adams plays no shot to Gus soon after and is leg before. And from the depths of 126 for six the previous day and cursing our luck over Smokes' run out, we have them 135 for six. Lara is gone, the Trini Posse is silent and Gus has taken three wickets for five runs in thirteen balls.

Curtly joins Williams and they put on thirty-odd. Bloody Curtly gets away with one from me that goes past his front pad and hits him plumb in front on the back leg, offering no shot. Sometimes you wonder why you bother. If the umpires are not going to give those out, what is the point?

BUT I get my first wicket of the tour when David Williams sweeps and misses at 167 for seven.

Gus is beaming as we leave the field and he has every right to do so. Five for 47 from thirteen overs and all five are proper wickets – Stuart Williams, Lara, Hooper, Chanderpaul, Adams. Brilliant.

Get back to the hotel feeling rather pleased with the day. Few beers etc as we are well back in the game. Get to the room for another early night as tomorrow will be crucial, then notice an absolutely horrific story in *Newsday*, that takes the wind out.

'Eight-year-old Jozanne Rojas died of massive head injuries on Wednesday, three days after being hit by a wheel that wrenched loose from a travelling water truck.

'The girl, of St Mary's village, Moruga, was involved in

The morning after ... my attempts to get over our defeat in the second Test in Trinidad revolved around beers, many fags, and Tia Marias.

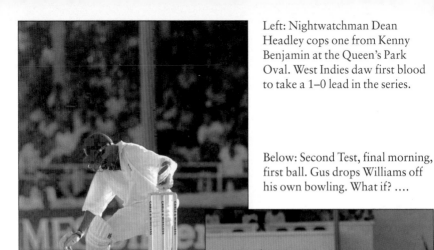

Left: Nightwatchman Dean Headley cops one from Kenny Benjamin at the Queen's Park Oval. West Indies daw first blood to take a 1–0 lead in the series.

Below: Second Test, final morning, first ball. Gus drops Williams off his own bowling. What if? ….

Below: All done in the worst possible taste. The Trini Possee are 'entertained' by a streaker during day one of the third Test match.

Right: Hi, Lisa! Celebrating in style after a memorable five days at the Queen's Park Oval.

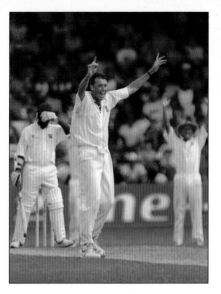

Above: Gus Fraser traps Lara lbw, the fourth time in four innings that he's taken the West Indies' most prized wicket. The home team are 102 for four and in deep trouble in the third Test.

Above: Butch makes up for his first ball duck in Jamaica by pulling Curtly Ambrose to the boundary in that tension-filled final day at Port-of-Spain, Trinidad in the third Test. A brilliant win for us to level the series 1–1.

Professor Lloyd examines his case notes on the last match. But why the crop circles?

The Iceman cometh to the Everest Ground, Georgetown.

The Spin Doctor and his patients. At Bourda, Robert Croft and I prepare to play a Test together for the first time in a year. John Emburey, our assistant coach, keeps his thoughts under his hat.

My complaints about umpires failing to give lbws against left-handers padding up have unexpected side-effects.

Funky chicken, groovy hat. Outside the Bourda Ground in Georgetown.

Vote ME for a brighter future – free fags for all and bowling to Brian Lara with 22 outfielders.

Above: The crowd invasion sparked by Chanderpaul's hundred in Guyana during the fourth Test left the pitch badly roughed up.

Below: 'HOWASSATTHATTHISTIMETHEN?' My 472nd unsuccessful appeal for an lbw decision. Is this a record?

Above: Cricket, lovely cricket. Lovely.

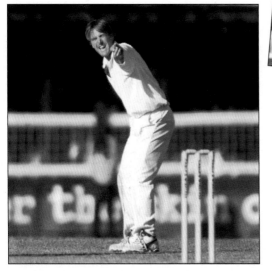

Right: Day Three of the fourth Test in Guyana, and a classy half century from Ramps in our first innings, in partnership with a brave No 11 (inset). I'm employing my 'Get out of the way of that ball, it hurts' technique against fast bowling.

Above: 'Anybody after seats? ... I've got two together on C branch.'

Below: Brian Lara never really tore us apart as he had in the past, but his was always the prize wicket.

the bizarre incident on the pavement outside her school, the St Mary's Government primary school.

'She had only just left her home and was heading towards a neighbourhood parlour to buy a phone card for her elder sister, when the tragedy took place...

'According to her older sister Giselle, the pretty little girl had come home from school that evening in a happy mood to greet her mother and two sisters.

'She ate a hearty meal, changed her clothes, took money from her sister and immediately set off for the shop to run the errand.

'Her parting word to Giselle was 'I going. I'll come back just now.'

'Minutes later, a neighbour brought the news that the girl was lying on the pavement.'

Hellfire. Talk about putting things in perspective.

Saturday 7 February, Second Test, Day 3

West Indies 1st inns 191 all out; England 2nd inns 219–4 (Thorpe 32*, Hollioake 9*)

We know exactly what we need to do. Root out the last few quick and cheap. Try and get a lead, even if it is only five or ten. Then crack on.

Gus obliges, quick and cheap. In nineteen balls he gets all three – Benjamin, then the dangerous Nixon McLean, and wraps it up with a cunningly disguised slower ball, ahem, against Curtly. In fact, Gus completely lost his run up and by the time he reached the crease all he could manage was a slow full toss. Amby, suitably flummoxed, patted back to him for a caught and bowled. They are out for 191, we lead by 23. Gus finishes with eight for 53, the best by an Englishman against West Indies, beating his own figures of eight for 75 against them in Barbados four years earlier. When he bowled Benjamin in the first over of the day, it was his 33rd wicket against West Indies in the Caribbean, another record for an England bowler, beating Jim Laker's 32. And he got McLean and Amby out in successive deliveries, so he's on a hat-trick next innings. He's chuffed, as he bloody well ought to be. By common consent there was no chance that he would have made the starting line-up had Darren Gough been fit to lead a three-man attack with Deano and Caddy, and even those who love him to bits thought he might have been struggling early on in the tour. But he has come through and he has done the job.

I'm reasonably pleased with my one for 33 from 20 overs but still slightly perturbed by the fact that the left-handers have decided to play football against me.

For the moment, everything is to do with getting a match-winning score. Athers and Alec bat brilliantly, taking on Walsh and Amby and cashing in on a pitch which plays better now on the third day than at any time. Has the sun dried up the surface? There is less and less uneven bounce now and almost no sideways movement. That means batting is easier but it also means we must get plenty, not only to give ourselves the best chance to win but also to make sure we can't be caught.

Athers is unlucky to drag one on, but Alec is fluent and in charge. The fall of Alec's wicket is a disappointment but, for any impartial observers, the incident in question has to be the champagne moment of the match so far. Al edges a quick one from Nixon McLean through to David Williams behind the stumps. The ball flies straight through his gloves, bounces off the middle of his forehead and dollies up behind him to where Hooper takes the rebound. When he comes round, Williams claims an 'assist'.

Creeps follows soon afterwards, but then Nass and Chalks get together and start to pull the game away from them.

Then, before they can really do so, another slice of bad luck ends their partnership when Nass is caught and bowled by Courtney from the *seventh* ball of an over. Bucknor, the umpire at the bowler's end has lost count, but the official scorers up in the press box, including our own Malcolm Ashton, are waving frantically to attract his attention. Bucknor fails to notice, Venkat makes no move and Nass hits what may have been a bump-ball catch back to Walsh. Nass is unaware of the unlucky seventh when he gets back to the dressing-room but is still unsure as to whether he hit the ball into the ground and asks: 'Was that out?'. He is told yes and no. We think it was a clean catch, but, er … it was the seventh ball of the over … DUCK!! Nass is not, as they say, best pleased.

Nevertheless, with Chalks and Smokes there at the close at 219 for four, a lead of 242 with six wickets remaining, we are in with a great chance. Whatever else, it's now in our hands.

Everyone realises the significance of what we can achieve here. They have been thrashed in Pakistan 3-0, this is Lara's first authentic Test in charge and it is on his home territory. If we can just finish the job, we are set up for the series and they will have to chase us. Sleep very well.

Sunday 8 February, Second Test, Day 4

England 2nd inns 258 all out; West Indies 2nd inns 181–5 (Hooper 40*, Williams, D 36*)
Hopes are high.

Certainly the *Trinidad Guardian* believes all we really have to do to win is turn up.

Under the headline 'WINDIES FACE GRIM PROSPECT', Fazeer

Mohammed writes: 'The 59-year-old fortress of the Kensington Oval came crumbling down at English feet in 1994. The 21 years of West Indian invincibility in Tests at the Queen's Park Oval may not be nearly as impressive, yet an end to that record will be another worrying signpost in the recent journey of West Indies cricket.

'The navigators seem to have lost the road map that leads back to discipline, consistency and dominance.'

No-one is taking anything for granted, but at the start of the day the mood is upbeat, to say the least, and we begin reasonably enough. There are no precise targets, but if we can just add another 100, a target of 340–350 must surely be beyond them.

The one thing on our minds is that we must not allow ourselves to get blown away. Eighty minutes later, however, that is precisely what has happened. Do NOT mention the 46. Try Curtly Ambrose: five wickets for sixteen runs in forty-seven deliveries.

It has to be said that we do not get the rub of the green with a couple of umpiring decisions, says Mandy Rice Tufnell. No, honest.

After Smokes nicks a good one at 228 for five, Jack gets a shocking leg before decision against him off a ball that pitches outside leg stump and would have missed off, 238 for six. Chalks drives and edged Courtney to Lara in the slips, 239 for seven. Caddy, is given out caught behind, didn't hit it, too bad, 239 for eight and Gus goes at 246 for nine and Christ!, I'M IN NEXT!

On a king pair. Bit fretful, but decide that if I'm going down I'm going down fighting.

Now anyone who thought I was taking guard some way outside leg stump in order avoid getting hit by the hard ball, five point penalty, full question to St. Todger's. Me. Philip

Tufnell. Trampling all over the square leg umpire in order not to get hurt. With my reputation? As any student of my batting technique should be only too aware, this particular method is known as 'giving myself room to play a few shots through the offside'. Viv Richards used to do this often and who am I to argue with the masterblaster?

Anyway, with a bit of good fortune I manage to slog a few and we finish up on 258 all out. Not what we wanted and we are well pissed off that, from having them down and dirty we have allowed them back in the game.

BUT, we have the score. They need 282 on a track that is still doing a little, with the odd one keeping low, and they will have to bat extremely well to get them. We are a little shaken, but we are still very confident we can do this.

Vital to strike early, or at least restrict their openers so that 282 looks a long way off. But Deano and Caddy will be the first to admit that they do not use the new ball well. Although Stuart Williams goes cheaply, Campbell and Lara take them past 50 without much alarm and get a little momentum going.

You have to bowl arse-grippin' tight at a time like this to make the opposition think they have nowhere to go. But we bowl a little short and a little loose and pay the price. Then, suddenly, we all look up at the scoreboard and they are only 200 away from winning the match.

For the first time I get this nasty little wobbly irritation that this might all be slipping away.

But cometh the hour, cometh Gus. I have the greatest respect for Lara as a batsman and a person. He's made the highest score by anyone ever in Test cricket, 375 against England in 1994, and on their last tour to our place he smacked millions. But if he was at the wicket now, with West Indies chasing 282 to win the second (unscheduled) Test match at the Queen's

Park Oval, Port-of-Spain, Trinidad and Tobago, and he started trying to slap Gus to all parts of the arena, I would say to him: 'Oi. Lara. No. You do not do that to Angus Fraser.'

Very shortly after the big man enters the action, he snares Lara again for seventeen at 67 for two. Big celebrations. Huge relief. Immense moment.

Genuine belief that we have removed the great obstacle to victory. All due respect and so forth, but when you get right down to it, really, the picture is this: get Stuart Williams, Hoops, Chanderpaul and Adams and we must have them and how that would set us up for the whole series.

Still work to be done, though. Hoops and Williams make some progress, and as they do, so the tension begins to mount again. No secrets, we see cool Carl as the big danger man, the one with the ability to just flatten you with strokes. They put on 53, every run chipping away at the target and at your sense of well-being.

It is so tense. The heat. And the drums. Those blasted drums. Will they ever stop?

JEEZUS, what was that? Williams has clipped Gus off the middle of the bat towards mid-wicket and Creeps has PLUCKED IT OUT OF THIN AIR. You beauty! 120 for three. Gus has his tenth wicket of the match. Come on.

Okay, settle down. Don't try and force it. Concentrate.

My turn, bowling to Chanderpaul, next over. Keep it tight, keep the pressure on. Not like that, you prat ... I've gone and pulled one down short. Idiot. Hold up. Chanderpaul tries to turn it off his hips, gets a leading edge and Chalks, running backwards at silly point, grabs it. 121 for four. Come on! Just Adams and Hooper now. Come on!

Next over, Gus gives Adams a little chance to drive ... edge ... slow-motion ... Stewie takes it at second slip. Now then. 124 for five. Three wickets for five runs in no time at all.

Hoops now. Just bloody Hoops ... then David Williams the keeper, then Amby & co. and we are there.

Steady. Don't clutch. Remember the plan and stick to it. Give them nothing. Hoops is the only one who can win this for them now; tie him up bowling over the wicket into the rough outside his leg stump, so that if he wants to score he must take risks, let the seamers chip away at the other end and let's get the beers in. Only a matter of time. No disrespect, but we fancy David Williams and the rest should be history.

Here we go. Williams, on about ten, steps right across his stumps and is hit on the pads in front of middle and off. He's so far across that not only is the leg stump visible to the umpire but so is middle as well. THIS IS IT. Huge shout. Stick your bloody finger up Stevie B...

Mr Bucknor declines. How big a moment will this become?

You never come out and say it, of course, but to ourselves we are all asking the same question: 'Sorry, but how was that actually not going to hit the stumps?'

Calm down. Keep at it. It WILL come. We've got him once. We'll get him again. Hold it together. Stick to the plan.

As time progresses, however, concerns and tension grow again. They do not seem to be in a great deal of difficulty. Are we getting tired? Are we a shade ring rusty? Is the pitch easing? Probably yes, yes and yes.

Hoops looks serene, Williams jumps about a bit, but more or less everything is clumping into the middle of his bat as well.

Is the plan right? Should I be bowling around the wicket to Hoops and challenging him to take me on? I feel as though I should at least have a go and I make enquiries, but Athers chats with Nass and Stewie and the consensus is no, stick to the plan. Do not panic. The plan is right. The plan will work.

Plan or no plan, I'm still not entirely happy with my bowling. Going over the wicket is something I can do – and this is not the first time I have done it for England by a long chalk – but it is not *what* I do. Just feel as though I am not getting into any kind of dangerous rhythm. Okay, they are not hitting me. In fact, Hoops has decided to not even bother. But am I taking the game anywhere? Am I applying any pressure?

For instance, there are a couple of overs I send down to Hoops where absolutely nothing happens. I pitch the ball wide of the leg stump into the rough, he lets the ball turn and hit him and we carry on. I feel as though I might as well not have bowled them at all.

The day ends flat for us, as it started. Somehow, Williams has hit his way to 36 and Hoops is not out 40. That lbw is on everyone's minds. The pitch is deadening, nothing much is doing and they need 101 to win with five wickets remaining.

Get back to the room to ponder and wonder. Lisa rings from home: 'Hard luck, darling. Well bowled. Keep at it. Oh, by the way, they've been saying on the radio that you should be bowling around the wicket to Hooper.' Without knowing it, Lisa has just taken five and half feet off my height.

Then I get angry. What do they know? Are they out there bowling their butts off?

Maybe they're right, though. Maybe they ARE right. Oh, bloody hell. Why didn't Bucknor give that lbw against Williams? If he had done, we would have been through to Curtly, the game might have been over by now, and the plan would have worked perfectly.

Am I bowling okay? Should I be bowling around the wicket? Should I press the point tomorrow? Oh, sod it. I'm going around the wicket tomorrow. Who is Carl Hooper anyway? Even if he takes me on, he's still got to middle the thing. He might cart me out of the ground, but he might equally well slog one up in the air.

But am I bowling with enough aggression? Am I being nasty enough out there? To be honest, there are times when I feel that I am just not getting the ball to the other end.

There may be a physical reason for this. Because the seamers, and Gus in particular, are striking from the pavilion end, I've been designated the press box end, from which bowling appears to me to be slightly uphill. The sighting is not great either. Behind the end I'm bowling at, the frame of the pavilion is miles back beyond the boundary and another fifty yards further behind the cycle track. I can't seem to *see* the target properly.

Or is this all crap?

Oh my God. Here we go again. Five wickets to get with a countdown. Why can't playing for England ever be simple? This is ripping my guts out.

Monday 9 February, Second Test, Day 5

West Indies 2nd inns 282–7 (Hooper 94*, Benjamin 6*).
West Indies win by 3 wkts. West Indies 1, England 0
Nervous? With my reputation?

Too bloody right, I'm nervous. I wake up with nothing in my mind except Hoops and Williams. Everywhere I look in the room, at breakfast, on the bus to the ground … in my head all I can see is those bastards.

At the start of the day, the message is clear and strong from Athers and Bumble. Be patient. Don't push it. We are still going to win.

By the end of the day, just after lunch in fact, the message has long been forgotten.

The nightmare starts with the first ball of the day. Gus bowls a loosening full toss to David Williams which he spoons straight back at him. Off balance and not expecting such a result from such a crap ball, Gus dives, reaches but cannot cling on .

Down at fine leg I'm not sure at first whether it is a catch or even whether it has carried. But the reactions of everyone else, all nearer to the action than me, tell the tale. It's a drop.

Next up, Jack, diving full stretch down the leg side to another Williams flick off the hip from Gus, just can't keep hold of the ball. There is no signal of leg bye from Bucknor so that is another life for Williams.

Having checked with the chaps about bowling over or round the wicket, the message remains: stick to the plan, keep it tight and let Gus chip away from the other end ... and then Gus traps Williams in front for the second time, in almost identical fashion to yesterday's near-miss. This time ... come on, Stevie B ... this time. Get your bloody finger up, man. NOT this time. Is this going to be one of those days?

Now, slight change of plan. Gus needs a breather, so I take over from him at the pavilion end, the first time I have had a go from this end in the match. Suddenly, this feels better. I go around the wicket and there is pace on the ball at last. I'm no longer heaving the ball down the other end, but gliding it and it is hitting the deck and gathering. This is better ... and now I GET WILLIAMS!

He pushes forward with the bat behind the pad, but the front leg is rigid, not bent at the knee, and the ball flips through the top of the pad onto his glove and balloons up for Chalks to take the catch at silly point. Yeees!!

Everyone is going mental. NOW WE MUST BE THROUGH.

But ... why isn't Williams walking off? I look around at

106

Bucknor for confirmation, but he is motionless. Has he already given him? No, he can't have done, or Williams would be on his way. Don't say he's not given it. Don't say it. He has *not* given it.

Hold on a minute. How many lives is that for Williams? Two leg befores against Gus that we are certain are dead. Gus's drop, Jack's half-chance and now this. Five lives. Five. Wait a sec, another shout from Smokes for one that is hitting everything. Six now. Is this bloke ever going to get out?

Hoops, completely unfazed, is milking us, the target is diminishing. We are trying hard, but by now a few of the lads are sensing that this is just not going to be our day. Time slips by and runs leak. The new ball is due, so off I come at the top end for Gus to have one last crack. He has two more plumb lbw shouts against Williams, but by the fourth time of asking we're not even looking for the answer.

When Williams is finally out, our chance of winning has become remote. Amby doesn't last, but by lunch they need next to bugger all. The interval is like a 40 minute stay of execution.

Then the axe falls just afterwards in suitably anti-climactic fashion. Hoops has slapped a couple, then a ball goes through Jack and hits a fielder's helmet on the ground behind him for five runs. Just about sums up our perfect day.

No question, Hoops has played magnificently. His 94 not out has won the match and I doubt if anyone on the ground, including the Windies supporters, really believed he was going to do it. So often they have seen him bat as though he invented the game, then infuriate them by getting out lazily, casually, sometimes suicidally.

Now all those times are instantly forgiven.

We trudge off, bewildered. How did we lose that? How?

Handshakes for them. They can't take it in either, I don't

think. But once we get into our dressing-room, it is a morgue. Four or five of the blokes are sitting there with towels over their heads, unable to speak. And now we have to go out for the presentation ceremony.

I retire to the showers and resolve to drown myself.

Bit of a rumpus outside, apparently, when some pissed-up member starts having a go at Athers. Gus and Stewie intervene, then the bloke is dragged away by his mates. Slight embarrassment when Athers is called up by Bob Willis to say a few words, but Athers doesn't hear him and stays put in his seat in front of the dressing-room. Eventually someone informs him and he shuffles along. Willis asks him for his thoughts. He says that it was a poor pitch, but that sometimes poor pitches produce great matches. But his first words are the ones that the crowd fasten onto and they start to jeer. Does anyone need all this?

Come out of the shower, eventually. Grab a beer and light one up. Then it hits. Knowing that you have had the game in your hands and then let it go is without doubt the worst of all possible feelings. Far easier to take if you are hammered out of sight.

Don't hang around at the ground. Just want to disappear.

Around the lightning-shaped pool a group has formed, including a few players: Embers, dispensing multitudinous theories as usual, and most of them, as usual, correct; the Sky commentators, Beefy, Paul Allott, Mark Nicholas and a couple of the press guys. Lots of white wine consumed and lots of chat about what went wrong.

Did we treat Hoops with too much respect? Did we stop playing the game and start playing him? Did we sit back and wait a little, rather than going out and fetching the game? More wine and more navel-gazing. Should I have bowled around the wicket more? What about the leg before decisions … and the catches? And how many lives did Williams want? Sod this. Nothing is being resolved here and the booze is not dulling the pain. 'Beef' takes me off to his room for some gigantic Scotches. He is brilliant, knows exactly what I am thinking but haven't quite got around to saying, and he tells me NOT to blame myself. The plan was good. We stuck to it. On this occasion, it just didn't quite come off. Does he really believe it, though? Do I?

I cannot get away from thinking I didn't do the job that I do for Middlesex day in/day out, namely, win the match.

Later we reconvene at the Pelican Bar down the hill where the atmosphere is a bit like a guilt convention. Everyone is blaming themselves. Me, Deano for not bowling well, even Smokes for not putting on enough runs on the Sunday morning.

Later, the booze converts guilt to depression, then to irrational anger, mainly directed at the umpires, viz. we all know that there is no point in moaning about umpires and that they have a difficult job to do and that bad decisions are part and parcel of the game, but does anyone sit them down in front of a video and ask 'Why was that not out?' Here ends the rant.

I am shattered. The adrenalin that keeps you going on the field has drained and I can barely move. I'm struggling to get into the drink now as well. Too tired. Too sad.

Athers and Lara come face to face. They get on well, which is fortunate, but Ath gives Lara a hard time along the lines of 'You lucky bastard. We were the better side.' Sensibly he stops short of saying 'We hammered you. We know it and you know it', but Lara takes it all in great good humour. Why wouldn't he? He's the winner in his home town in his first proper Test match as captain. Walsh, Jamaica, Sabina Park and Pakistan must seem a billion miles away.

Later, Ath becomes insensible with drink, leans and tries to support his weight by placing one hand on a nearby table. Like Del Boy in the famous bar room scene, he misses, keels sideways and hits the deck at pace. It takes him several minutes to rise.

How long will it take the rest of us?

CHAPTER SEVEN

Ruuuuuuunn...

Tuesday 10 February

Oh my God. My head. Who staved my head in with a shovel?
And who emptied the contents of every single ash-tray in
Port-of-Spain into my mouth? Bastards. Someone is going to
pay for this.

I ache everywhere and I feel like crap.

So a fax of the article written by Robert Crampton in *The
Times* Weekend section, resulting from our meeting in Mo
Bay, is just what I need.

During an interview lasting half an hour he has, of course,
discovered everything there is to know about me. The
content is derogatory and the tone is snide, but I've come to
expect nothing less from this type of so-called writer. I later
gather that when it was put to him that the piece appeared
to have been written from a preconceived notion, not to
mention his newpaper's cuttings library, with sod-all new
material, he claimed he had not had sufficient time to work
with me. Rubbish. I know for a fact that he was due to stay
longer but brought forward his flight because he couldn't
wait to get home.

What really upsets me is that I have gone and put myself
out for this bloke, not only in agreeing to do the interview in

the first place but getting up early on that Sunday morning so we can go and take some pictures to go with it. He has made absolutely no effort to get into what I am like now. Instead, it is the same old stuff. I am an easy target and, to be honest, I'm getting a bit sick and tired of it. Everything in my life seems to be inflated or deflated.

Decide to get out of the hotel and accompany co-author and our half-man half-dog creature, photographer Winston 'Muttley' Bynorth, to Maracas beach and beyond. When we get there for some postcard-type snaps of sun, sea and sand, it is, inevitably, pouring with rain and blowing a gale. Perhaps the most significant photograph taken is one of me sitting in a track in the middle of nowhere reading a newspaper whose front-page lead headline is 'HOMOS, LESBIANS ON THE RISE', while wearing a Dickie Henderson hat and having my personal space encroached upon by a rather large and rather obvious bull. Spend the rest of the day in a restaurant halfway up a mountain overlooking the ocean, eating fish and drinking large Tia Marias with ice. I don't even like Tia Maria. Or at least I didn't. Like the captain's behaviour the night before, this is called getting the Test match out of your system.

Realise that this is the first time I have seen a beach since we left rain-sodden Antigua a month ago. And apart from a half-hour visit to listen to the pan drummers on the Savannah the other night, almost everything we have done out here has been geared to the cricket. A lot of folks back home think that a tour of the Caribbean means a three-month holiday in the sun, drinking bathtubs of rum punch and slapping on the lotion, with a few matches thrown in along the way. That may have been the case in the dim and distant but it isn't now. The intensity of what we do is so great that any time we happen to have off is normally spent trying to repair the body. It's good to try and get free from the cricket from time to time, but the fact is that you never really do. It's in your mind all the time.

Wednesday 11, February

Pain, pain go away.

The press boys have jumped on some comments from Athers and Bumble reviewing what happened last week. The gist of Bumble's assessment is that although Gus and I did our jobs with the ball, we did not have a great deal of support from Deano and Caddy. He says: 'We lost because two key players under-performed big-time. Headley was playing his fourth Test, so is quite inexperienced. But that is not the case with Caddick – I'm sure he has plenty of theories as to why he bowled poorly. Phil Tufnell had to support Angus by blocking one end, because the other two bowlers were going for too many runs. The players know we should have won – and they know why we didn't. I logged every ball. Fraser bowled 70 per cent in the right place. Caddick and Headley much fewer. I expect international bowlers to put the ball in the correct place more often than that.'

Slightly surprised that the coach has been quite so pointed about what went on, but he must have his reasons. Caddy responds: 'These sorts of things should be private between me and the management. But it has been said and done and I will just get on with it.'

Caddy has often had a bad press outside the dressing room, and occasionally inside. But this will hurt him. He tries very hard to think the best of everyone and has a very generous nature. If anything practical needs sorting out, he is the original handy man. When the ear-piece on your discman is buggered, he'll fix it. If your telly's on the blink, he'll fix it. If you can't get the old studs out of your boots, he'll appear with a telescopic stud remover and in a flash your boots will be re-studded and better than ever. But this openness means he is a tad more sensitive than others. I suppose Bumble is trying to gee him up with his comments. It will be interesting to see how he responds.

Athers's criticisms are more general. 'We played as if we believed the game would fall into our laps. But that doesn't happen in Test cricket.

'Maybe everyone simply expected the remaining West Indies wickets to fall, rather than making them fall. That's no good. You must keep working to drive home the advantage.'

Day brightened considerably by a story in the local paper concerning a bungled attempt at cocaine smuggling by a Ugandan named Cassoulet. According to police sources, he was apprehended while trying to board a plane and after a search was found to be carrying two big bags of cocaine. A police officer explained the reason Cassoulet was suspected of being up to no good as 'an unusually large bulge in the area of his groin.' I see.

Thursday 12 February

Got to snap out of it now. Tomorrow, we go again. A couple of days reflecting has not done much good, but maybe it has not done any harm either. We are so up for it now and so desperate to make amends and show that we can win here, and the great thing is that we do not have long to wait.

In fact, we all realise we simply must win. To go 2–0 down here would be the cue for the fat lady. A lot of people are writing us off, doubting our fibre and all that. The first question they ask is this: if we couldn't win a match like the last one when it was in our hands, when are we going to win one? The second is, notwithstanding the high-seam balls which have enabled Gus to grip and rip, will we get them in a similar position again?

At the team meeting we run through a few of the positive things that came out of our defeat and the message is this: we got into a position to win the game once, so we can do it again. Bumble drives it into us that we had the winning of the game and that this time we've just got to go out and nail it. Above all, we must prove to ouyrselves and everyone else that we are not just another bunch of losers.

Bad news for Smokes, though. His back is hurting badly. He first felt it in the match at Guaracara Park when he was bowling. That was the first time he tried to do so since injuring his shoulder in the match against West Indies 'A' at Chedwin Park. He has a slingy action anyway but in favouring the shoulder at the oil refinery ground he might have twisted something which has then got worse and worse. Although he played in the last Test, he struggled when bowling. In fact, he said to me that after his first spell he was hoping Athers wouldn't ask him to have another go as he felt he simply wouldn't have been able to. From time to time he is just seizing up, and now it is touch and go for him. Always a dodgy area, this. Everyone is dying to get on the field and often you play through little niggling injuries, but you owe it to your team-mates to go out there fit and able to play. There is more to it than simply trying to get through. Smokes is hugely frustrated. Strong bloke, desperate to get going to try and establish himself in the Test side, but nothing is really going for him. If Smokes is not fit, Ramps must have a great chance of taking his place at number six.

The other slightly less serious business to come out of the team meeting is the latest series of fines for wearing the wrong gear. I was done for the wrong shoes, or the wrong facial expression or something, and all this is getting a bit out of hand. Our suppliers are the clothing firm Asics and our sponsors are Vodafone. Some of the shirts have one logo on and some have both. There are blue Asics tops and blue Vodafone tops and sometimes we have to wear one and not the other, and there are grey Asics and grey Vodafone and the blue shirts have got a bit of grey in them and the grey shirts have got a bit of blue in them, and it's doing my head in. Nass and Chalks, who had been put in charge of dress codes, have resigned. Who can blame them? Why can't someone just give us six blue shirts with nothing on and have done with it? It would certainly make touring cheaper for me.

Friday 13 February, Third Test, Queen's Park Oval, Day 1

Close of play: West Indies 1st inns 159 all out; England 1st inns 22–2 (Stewart 16*, Headley 1*)

A most bizarre story has come to its conclusion. Local television newscaster Vaughn Salandy died at 9.45 pm last night and the papers this morning are full of the news. Last Sunday, Salandy who had travelled to Barbados 'under mysterious circumstances' called the front desk at the Accra Beach hotel just outside Bridgetown seeking medical help after informing them he had taken a weed-killer called gramoxone.

According to the *Trinidad Independent*: 'When contact was made with his employers, the Caribbean Communications Network in Port-of-Spain, a decision was taken to fly him home under the care of toxologist Dr Edward Addo.

'A mix-up on Monday evening caused him to miss his flight out of Grantley Adams International airport and forced a postponement of his return to Tuesday. An air ambulance was chartered as an alternative, but a rainstorm in Puerto Rico on Tuesday morning further delayed the process.'

And by the time he arrived in Trinidad just after 11 am on Tuesday, the deterioration in his condition was apparently irreversible.

According to Dr Addo: 'The three-day lapse in commencement of his treatment was the significant factor.'

Salandy gave no reason for his actions. But the psychologists queued up. Dr Jillian Ballantyne commented: 'The reality of suicide is that the higher a man is on the social ladder in terms of success etc, the more likely he is to attempt suicide, because he can't handle failure or any setback.'

Sometimes I'm very glad I'm just a bloke who can bowl a bit of left-arm spin.

And now, back to the cricket.

For both Smokes, and then, would you believe it, poor old Ramps, Friday the thirteenth is all that it is cut out to be. Smokes has a fitness test and is ruled out as he thought he might be, but Ramps has not even made it to the ground. The flu virus that has laid most of us low at regular intervals on the trip has absolutely wasted him. He is laid out in bed at the hotel, barely able to walk let alone play a Test match.

So Butch gets another chance. We were all hoping that his tour would consist of more than just his first-ball dismissal at Sabina Park, and now it won't.

Life and soul, Butch. Apart from his all-singing, all-guitar-playing karaoke specials, he is our style guru. There's nothing particularly a la mode about spending three months carrying out the drinks, however, and he will be very keen to put *that* ball behind him.

Getting focused now and helped somewhat by the back-page headline in the *Trinidad Independent* above an article by Colin Croft, former VERY fast West Indies bowler and a man with whom, in normal circumstances you probably would not argue. It reads: 'ENGLAND HAVE NO CHANCE.' Get off the fence, Crofty. For God's sake, say what you mean.

The pitch looks better than the last one, but there is obvious damage where the bowlers have run off the other wicket next door. No-one is quite certain what to do should we win the toss. The wise men have all had a look and had their say, but they have all reached different conclusions so no definite plan of action has been formed. I think Athers is looking for a little inspiration when he goes out to toss.

He wins it and decides that we will have a bowl this time. Maybe a touch of greenness and moisture has persuaded him, but it is obviously a big risk because if nothing happens early on and they build a total, we will be 1–0 down and chasing the game.

What happens next totally vindicates the gamble.

It doesn't look that way at first. Sherwin Campbell and Stuart Williams get off okay and though Williams is out at 36 for one, Lara and Campbell again tuck into Caddy. At lunch they are 72 for one. Not the first morning collapse Athers was hoping for. Then, straight after the break, sodding carnage. First over after lunch, Lara smashes three to the boundary, Campbell follows the leader and nineteen are taken. In seconds, it seems, they are 93 for one and we are just starting to get a tad twitchy.

Then, just as he did in the first match here, Gus becomes a thing of the greatest beauty.

All right boys, just give the ball to me now and perhaps we can start the game.

In his first over, Campbell edges Gus to Chalks at slip. 93 for two. Gus's next over, Hooper, 94 not out last time, slashes a drive square of the wicket and Butch, leaping up and back like Nureyev, clutches onto the ball one handed. GREAT catch. 95 for three. Massive relief after what he did to us last time, and now the sniff of a chance. But Lara is still there, the sun is shining, the Trini Posse is swinging…

And Gus goes and does it again.

Just short of a full length, certainly not short enough to pull, Lara sways and aims to crack him through mid-wicket, gets a thin under edge and the ball dips on its way through to Jack. Jack scoops it, we all appeal. Time stands still, again.

Now, two things need to be sorted. One: did he hit it? We are sure he did. Two: Did it carry? Jack is sure it did. But the umpires are not. Indeed the man at the bowler's end, Eddie Nicholls, the Guyanese standing in his first Test, seems unsure on both counts. He hesitates. Who wouldn't? This is going to be a crucial decision. Nicholls peers appealingly across to Darrell Hair, the big cheery Aussie standing at square leg. Hair sort of takes the initiative to get to the bottom of both questions. On the face of it, Nicholls's look at him seems to suggest he only wants to know if the ball has gone clean into Jack's gloves. But is he really saying: 'For Christ's sake, I don't know, but this is soooo important that we cannot be wrong. Third umpire, help, please.'?

Third umpire Cumberbatch, the same man who got Hollioake's run out wrong last week, is under pressure himself. But, this time, after watching the incident upside down, inside out, slow motion, normal speed, Keystone Kop, you name it, he gives the decision. Lara is out. Gus has three wickets for spit in three overs. And West Indies are 100 for four.

Now all the misery of last week is forgotten. We are IN this game. Just Chanderpaul and Adams (and Williams?) to get and we are among them again. This bloody game does it to you every single time.

We hold it together. They struggle to hit the ball off the square. 93 for one just after lunch. At tea they are 127 for four. The order is: strangle the batsmen. I'm on with Gus. Give them nothing. Give them nothing.

What on earth is that? Oh, brilliant. Here we are, nerves taut to breaking point and some big fat ugly English cow has run onto the pitch starkers except for a Trinidad and Tobago flag, trying to make a name for herself. After removing the flag she then bares all to the members. What a sight. Get off the pitch. And don't come back.

Get the focus back quickly, don't lose the moment. Luckily we don't. After tea, Caddy gains his revenge for everything the West Indies batsmen have done to him and all that has been said about him. Four wickets in seven balls. Adams, fantastic catch by Athers at short cover, big drive, one hand, safe. Then Williams, our other stumbling block last week, is beautifully yorked first ball. (Williams and Hooper have made one run between them. How typical is that?). Caddy's next over misses the hat-trick but doesn't have long to wait. Ambrose is bowled and then Kenny Benjamin leg before, absolutely dead. They are 140 for eight.

Now then. Now then.

Fraser finishes them off, Chanderpaul, leg before and Nixon McLean a skied catch to Deano in the deep. 150 all out. Gus has taken five for 40 and Caddy five for 67. Can you believe it? Can you believe it?

Whatever happens now, there is going to be a result. If we can get a lead, anything, we can control the match. But this time, this time, we must win the bloody thing every single ball. If we give ourselves a chance, we must take it. If we fail, we are done. So we must not fail.

Nipping them out so early means that there is still work to be done today. Ath goes cheaply, leg before to Amby for two and Creeps is bowled for one. Deano goes out as nightwatchman and we finish 22 for two.

A breathless day. What's in store for tomorrow? More tension. More gut-wrenching, arse-pinching tension. What a way to earn a living. Dressing-room attendant lightens the load slightly. He is old and wizened and had his day made by the wobbly one. 'I ain't seen that sort of ting for some years, man,' he explains, 'she comin' again tomorrow?'

Saturday 14 February, Third Test, Day 2
England 1st inns 145 all out; West Indies 2nd inns 71–2 (Lara 30*, Benjamin 0*)
The rollercoaster ride continues. Deano is out without addition to give Amby the figures of three wickets for four runs from seven overs. Ooo-er. Forty-six all out. What 46 all out? And the nerves start to jangle again when, minutes later, Nass gets his second strange dismissal in a row. Out off the seventh ball last time he went in to bat here, this time he plays and misses by a mile at a ball from Courtney and is given out caught behind.

He just about manages to keep things together, but bearing in mind this makes us 27 for four, finds it hard. A few glances upwards then a slow walk back to the hutch say it all, and television replays show he was nowhere near the ball. When he gets back, we all make for cover again. The list of decisions that have gone against us is growing uncomfortably long.

So far on this tour, we have all stuck pretty well to the no-whinge approach outlined before we set off. Whingeing creates negative energy, so the theory goes, and negative energy is, well, negative.

121

Yes. But sometimes it doesn't half help to let off steam. Nass is doing columns for the *Mail On Sunday*, with which he is assisted by my co-author, their cricket correspondent. Not unnaturally, Nass is contacted during the day by his ghost writer to see if he wants to say anything about a) the decision and b) the fact that he has now had two peculiar dismissals in a row.

In a mobile phone call across the ground, probably routed via satellite halfway across the globe, Nass says: 'I don't know what you can and what you cannot print, but all I really want to say is that I didn't hit it. I was nowhere near the ball and I'm pissed off. I don't want to slag off the umpire because we all make mistakes. It's a bloody difficult job and no-one gets things wrong deliberately. But the fact is that I didn't get a touch.'

Hayter believes that as long as Nasser is seen not to be criticising Eddie Nicholls the umpire, it is fair comment for him to give his version of what took place. However, according to our tour contracts whatever Nasser writes or whatever appears under his name has to be shown to our Media Relations Manager Brian Murgatroyd, who insists that the words 'I didn't hit the ball' are removed. Nass has no choice but to comply and Hayter, reluctantly, agrees. Seems a bit odd that Hansie Cronje, the captain of South Africa, can put a stump through the Australian dressing room door and get off scot-free, yet Nass is prevented from saying 'I did not hit the ball', when he clearly didn't. Nice to see that freedom of speech is alive and well.

I digress. With Nass out, it is up to Alec, Chalks, Butch, Jack and the tail to gather what they can. Irritatingly, it is not Walsh and Ambrose who now pile in, but their spinners, Hoops and Adams. To be fair, it is probably the pressure created by the quicks that encourages our boys to go for

122

their shots against the slow stuff, but Alec, Chalks and Butch are all out trying to cash in while they can. Butch hangs around and plays really well, especially for a bloke who had faced one delivery since September, at Sabina Park, and that a ball that nearly took his head off, Jack finishes with 20 not out, but this time the tail adds little. Philip Tufnell is out first ball, once again, but at least this time it was lbw, thus proving that I got right into line. Me. Philip Tufnell. Getting behind the line of the ball from one of the fastest bowlers in the world. On a sporting surface. With my reputation? Amby thus cleans up Gus and me in successive balls to finish with five for 25, the 20th five-wicket haul of his career. My mates don't believe me back home but it *is* pretty intimidating standing there against him even though I'm covered in enough padding to have kept the Titanic afloat, all designed to make sure that if he hits me it won't hurt too badly.

Bollocks. 145 all out, trailing by 14 runs. Once again our hearts are in our boots. Once again we had them, bowling them out for next to nothing, and once again we have let the advantage slip. It had better get better than this or we are going to slide down the swanee.

And it doesn't in the immediate. They finish the day 71 for two with a lead of 85. Why can't we just have a nice batting shoot-out; 400 plays 400. Tomorrow, I will be asked to bowl tight again and make sure they don't run away with things. My nerves, bashed enough already, are in for another pounding. We bowled on the first day of the Test, we bowled on the second day and now we are going to be bowling on the third. Could we please have a sodding break?

Get back to the hotel. Stare into space. Pick up today's newspaper and get slight nagging feeling that the date on top of the page should mean something. February 14, Febru-ary fourt ... Oh, Christ! It is Valentine's Day. Frantic fumbling for the phone and chaotic pushing of buttons. After several abortive attempts at dialling direct to England I finally succeed. Tone of voice at other end not encouraging. 'Oh. Hello, Philip. I was wondering when you might get around to ringing.'

In the same paper, I later notice an article quoting the lyrics of David Rudder's *High Mas*. I've heard the song so many times I could la-la it off by heart, but it's been impossible to decipher the words that the churchmen are objecting to. Now I know:

'Our Father, who has given us this art/ So that we can all feel like we are part/ Of this earthly (lesser) heaven/ Amen.

'Forgive us this day our daily weaknesses/ As we seek to cast our mortal burdens on this city/ Amen.

'And on this day when we come out to play and sway and do a little breakaway/ Some will say what they have to say/ But only you know the pain we are feeling/ Amen.

'As it was in the beginning of Jouvert/ Good vibes 'til carnival Tuesday/ Amen.

'Jah, be praised. Jah, be praised.

'O, the father, in his mercy/ Sends a little music to make the vibration raise/ So Carnival day, everybody come and celebrate/ See the ragamuffin congregate/ Everybody come and celebrate.'

Oh, well. I suppose sin is in the eye of the beholder.

Sunday 15 February, Third Test, Day 3

West Indies 2nd inns 210 all out; England 2nd inns 52–0 (Atherton 30*, Stewart 14*)
Ow. My hear hurts. Come to think of it, so does everywhere else.

Lord MacLaurin ('Ah, Tufnell, you *will* try not to get into any trouble, won't you?') has flown in to give his support to the boys. All good luck chaps and so on. Simon Pack, the International Teams Director, is also here asking everyone what they see as their role in the England set-up. As a military background implies, he is incredibly upright and proper in all things. Prone to lapsing into squaddiespeak from time to time as in 'we will r.v. at oh-eight-hundred-hours.(r.v. = rendezvous, of course). Invited someone to dine with him the other night and took his leave with 'Sups at 21 hundred, then'. Jolly good show. Awfully nice chap.

Not much said in the bus on the way to the ground. We know that every session is going to be crucial from now on. A maiden, or an over that goes for plenty could swing it. A stop in the field or a fumble, even down to singles, the match is going to be a proper perspiration producer. Do we have the bottle to take it this time?

We are all on a knife edge and what doesn't help is the cramped confinement of the dressing-room, not that we bowlers seem to have been able to stay inside it for very long. Slightly smaller than your average broom cupboard, this has been house and home for us and all our smelly kit for what seems like months. Every morning when we walk in it resembles a chinese laundry with gear draped everywhere, and we have long since given up trying to mark out any personal spaces. On more than one occasion, I have put on someone else's shirt, keks, socks without realising and if any one of us had been suffering from one of those nasty little skin irritations that single players tend to pick up on these tours, we would all have had it by now.

Grasping for any little thing to relieve the tension and find one such item in this morning's *Trinidad Independent*, in an article written by 'Dancing Brave' to 'educate the British scribes now in Trinidad.'

Nice to see the boys from Her Majesty's Press getting a spoonful or two of their own medicine, even if most of the content is completely baffling.

'What follows,' writes the Brave, 'are some corrections to those British Mongrels, using colloquial notations, where possible:

'Chris Lander, when you said England will win. Clearly you mean England's talent is thin. Also, when you spoke about a *Mirror* exclusive, maybe you ought to have said your views may be logic elusive.

'Alan Lee, surely, the West Indies players are not at odds with each other, what you should say is that England are not like any other. England, you should say, have no chance in this contest, it is only a matter of time before your selectors say 'Next! Next!'

'Is it true that Thorpe is England's number one? Because he looks more like somebody's number two.' Very nice.

'Michael Henderson, please understand Trinidad carnival is wonderful and should not be compared with England's carnival which is woeful. Also don't say Jack Russell is unlucky. What you mean is that Jack has to be happy that he is not playing cricket in Russia, otherwise he would be someone's Geisha.'

Sorry to interrupt, but I would appreciate your suggested answers on a postcard to that one, please.

'Simon Wilde, when you said something was wrong with the Oval pitch, what you really meant is that the West Indies bowled like a bitch. When you said Stewart should open maybe you meant Stewart is lucky not to be broken.'

'*The Evening Standard's* David Lloyd, when you said England would be back, did you forget England doesn't have the knack? Instead they look rusty with some players in need of the sack.'

'Mark Nicholas, instead of saying Fraser is great, you should have said Fraser is an ingrate. Instead of saying Fraser only dropped one catch you should have said Fraser cost England the match.'

'Anyway, my dear old English sods, I came across some fan mail.

'Hi Geoffrey Boycott, I really think that my left arm is more powerful than my right, because the last time I hit the bag, she, sorry, it, fell pretty hard and it looked to me like she had tripped.

'Jonathan Agnew, darling, I really love your accent on the radio. It turns me on and I only turn off the radio when you are not on. I live in Curepe and can cook, but not wash, but if you taste my curry, you will never want to leave. See you soon, My Valentine.'

Slightly more serious in tone comes a dire warning in the *T&T Express*.

'I, PASTOR SONA, was praying in my church one evening and GOD gave me a message to deliver to the people.

'God told me to let the people know that he is going to put his wrath upon this land because it grieved him to see that the people are turning away from him. The sin of this land has reached him. He is going to punish the people within three to four years from now. You will see the punishment of God upon the land, that is 2001 and 2002 years. After 1 and 2 years, that is 2003 and 2004 years you will see the punishment which will be very great upon this land. Thus saith the Lord thy God.

'TO PASTOR SONA OF THE TEMPLE OF GOD TACARIGUA.

'I am warning you people. The time will come when you will want God and you will not have him. It will be too late.'

I'm sure the moral of that message is as true today as it has ever been, but I'm somewhat more concerned with Sunday 15 February 1998 for the time being.

From their overnight position, with the game so far progressed already and time enough to finish it one way or another on a definite result pitch, Lara's boys must be favourites.

But the one thing that we are confident we can do is pull together as a team. And now we do it brilliantly.

Kenny Benjamin, the nightwatchman (what *does* that mean, exactly?) is out quickly, but we all know that if we are to stand any chance of winning, the guys we must remove cheaply are Lara and Hooper. By lunch we have them both.

What has got into Gus? Consistently excellent against all of them, he is currently Inspired against the great one and now he snares him for the fourth time in four innings. The ball might have hit Brian slightly high, but Hair thinks it's out and that's good enough. Maybe we are now getting the little bits of luck we did not have in the last Test. In any case, he's over and done with and you can almost see what a deflationary effect that has on their team and, just as importantly, their crowd.

The Trini Posse come to praise Lara, not to see him buried, and when he goes without giving them what they want they tend to quieten down somewhat. WHICH WE LOVE.

Hoops. Has the tide really turned? He gets a horrible shooter from Deano and is so out he almost walks and they are 102 for five.

We are on a white-knuckle journey that will not end.

Now another element. Jimmy Adams is without a Test fifty since he made 74 not out at Melbourne in December 1996 and has since been in an out of the side, but he chooses this of all moments to rediscover form. Clearly, our bowlers are tiring. The events of the past week or so have sapped everyone's strength, but are we going to be blocked again? Chanderpaul plays solid with Adams and I am again called upon to hold things together while the quicks take breathers.

I do the job, keep it tight and so forth, and in fact I end up conceding only thirteen runs from sixteen overs. But I want some bloody wickets to show for it and they are not coming.

Again Chanderpaul and Adams stand there with not the slightest intention of playing the ball but just kicking me away, and I'm getting a little bit sick and tired of it. One ball I bowl to Chanderpaul hits him on the back leg with him offering no stroke. It would have hit middle stump halfway up, but I almost feel that I am wasting my time in appealing for lbws.

If that one is not going to be given, someone is going to have to rewrite the bloody rules. The umpires are saying, in effect, that from over the wicket to the left-hander it is impossible for me to hit the stumps. And it is pissing me off.

And then we take control again and the feeling passes. Deano takes three wickets in seven balls; Chanderpaul, David Williams second ball and Curtly first and they are 159 for eight, a lead of only 173. Now it's coming. Just McLean and Walsh and we are through. This time. This time. Come on boys, one last big effort.

But now the bloody pendulum swings again. When will this ever stop? Lie down. Why can't you just lie down?

Adams, who is on just 14 when McLean arrives, farms the strike and with Nixon and Walsh he puts on another 51 bloody runs, making 39 of them himself. Every run, every leg-bye, bye, no-ball, anything increases the pressure. We are living every single second of this. There are no dead balls, no dead overs or passages of play. When a boundary is hit you can almost feel everyone dipping. It's getting a little crazy out here. The match is so tight. You feel like you cannot actually breathe properly. And the tension gets into your hands when you are bowling. My palms are now sweating so much with the heat and the anxiety that I'm having trouble gripping the ball. Only a game.

Nixon is out. Now only Walsh and we know he is ours. But he sodding isn't. The gangly scissor-arm shots are hilarious when they don't matter, but he is hanging around while Jimmy is just taking them into dangerous territory. It's hard to concentrate. We know that we are on the verge of the breakthrough that can set us up to win, but the pressure is just exhausting. And we are all knackered anyway.

Finally, we get Jimmy. Thank God for that. They are 210 all out, just 225 to win. Just 225.

The game is set up now. The sparring is over. It's a straightforward test of our batting against their bowling in the fourth innings of a Test on a pitch still giving assistance to the quicks. Anywhere else in the world against any other side, we would be confident of knocking these off, no bother. But against these guys there is always that feeling of trepidation. Four years ago, we had 194 to get and Curtly … don't mention the 46.

This is probably going to be the crucial session of the match, maybe the series. Twenty-five overs or so still to be bowled this evening and they will throw everything at us. Like they did four years ago. DON'T mention the 46.

The bowlers strip off, shower, try to relax. But it's no good.

The dressing-room is a complete mess. Dirty washing on backs of coffins, old cups of tea and coffee, bits of watermelon and curled up sandwiches. Not much is being said. You try and walk away from it for a few moments, but what is happening just draws you back, either to the telly or to the balcony. Young Ashley, all chirpy and upbeat, is swizzling around the dressing-room. Not now, Ash. Not now. And as Athers and Al start magnificently, silly little things start to creep in.

Old established superstition/tradition in all dressing-rooms is to stay put exactly where you are when a partnership is developing. All complete rubbish, of course, but you would be amazed how many times a wicket falls as a direct result of someone leaving their position in the dressing-room to go to the bog at the wrong time. Or coming back, for that matter. And you must never, ever, not ever say anything about what is going on out there. 'Athers is playing well' may not sound like careless talk, but almost invariably such a pronouncement is immediately followed by the sight of all three stumps cartwheeling out of the ground. AND IF YOU ARE THE ONE WHO HAS SAID IT, YOU ARE RESPONSIBLE.

Thus, I get up to go for a leak and everyone shouts: 'SIT DOWN!' The physio comes into the dressing-room from the balcony to get some spray and we all shout 'GET OUT!'

This kind of ritual is particularly closely adhered to during a countdown, and this is *the* countdown.

Athers and Al are batting superbly (I can say this now, as I am writing these notes after the close of play), Athers in some real form at last. The pitch, strangely, seems to have quietened down although the odd delivery is keeping low. But back in the dressing-room and outside, for the last twenty minutes of the day nobody moves a muscle.

They cruise through the session as though it's a Sunday club match. I'm not kidding, nothing misses the middle of the bat, and they come off at 52 for no wicket. Bearing in mind the pressure, this is an unbelievable performance. We could not have bought a better start. Beam me up. I don't think I can take much more of this. After this passage of play, however, with 173 to get , all pins standing and two days to go, now, perhaps, we won't have to. Perhaps.

We return to the hotel to crowds of England supporters cheering etc. 'You've got them now,' is their message. 'Thanks, but come and see us this time tomorrow,' is ours.

Where's my room? Where's my bed?

Monday 16 February, Third Test, Day 4
England 2nd inns 187–4 (Thorpe 15*, Butcher 9*)
We had all but forgotten about the streaker, but she hasn't half caused a furore here. The Archbishop, Anthony Pantin, describes the incident as lewdness while Jose Gomes writes to the *T&T Express*: 'The phenomenon of streaking is associated with sport in England and Australia, especially the game of cricket.

'We witnessed this in Trinidad for the first time during the third Test match when an ecstatic English fan decided to have some fun and create history here by being the first.

'Surely this woman should realise that she is a visitor to our country and should behave in a manner where she shows more respect to us as a nation and people. I think it would have been more fitting for her to run with the English flag rather than show this disrespect at a time when the match was being broadcast all over the world via television.

'She should be made to pay for this or to offer a public apology to the country. I hope she reads this and does not repeat this act anywhere else in the Caribbean.' Mr. Gomes had better have a word with our dressing-room attendant.

Arrive at the ground, all pumped up and full of everything. But looking round, I notice some funny looks on the faces of a few of my colleagues and then, looking up at the sky, I realise why.

Eight years ago, under Graham Gooch, four of our present squad – Alec, Jack, Gus and Nass – were here on their first tours. Completely against the odds and written off before they got here, they won the first match at Sabina Park, with Gus taking wickets. The second Test in Guyana was a wash-out, then they came to Trinidad and Devon Malcolm bowled West Indies to death, leaving England a paltry final innings target.

Gooch's team knew that if they managed to pull off a second victory several things were on the cards. Primarily, that result would ensure that the worst England could do was to draw the series, in itself a huge result against Viv's side rated then probably the best in the world. But the way they had been playing, it was unlikely that West Indies would have won both the remaining Tests in Barbados and Antigua and an incredible series win would more than likely have been in the bag. What is more, had England gone 2–0 up, the pressure on the home Board would have been so intense that they would almost certainly have brought forward their existing plans to bin some of the older players like Gordon Greenidge, Des Haynes, Malcolm Marshall and even Viv himself, thus making England's task that much easier.

But the dreams popped when first Goochie had his hand broken and then the rains came and stayed. After a couple of hours break, the boys eventually got back out, but the conditions were not really fit for play. The Windies boys slowed things down to such an extent that, with only another 31 runs wanted from 13 overs with five wickets remaining, bad light so bad that Jack could barely see his batting partner David Capel at the other end, forced them to call off the chase.

Quite apart from events here four years previously and

then again last week, what happened on this ground two tours ago has stuck in the craw of the three who played, Jack, Gus and Alec (Nass was not picked) ever since.

Why do I mention this now? Because although the ground is bathed in sunshine at the start, there are dirty great big black clouds assembling over the hills behind the far end of the ground.

Something equally alarming is happening in the Sandals pool area just beneath the main scoreboard. An Englishman with a white beard wearing only a pair of garish, brightly-coloured swimmers is standing in the pool with a mobile phone pressed to his ear and clutching a notepad and pen in his free hand. He is surrounded by a bevy of bathing beauties and he is having his photograph taken. And the Sky television close-ups show that he is also sweating profusely. At that moment the identity of this bizarre figure becomes clear. It is the ageing lothario, Chris Lander of the *Mirror*. 'What the f*** is he doing?'. Only later do we find out. The editor of his newspaper, Piers Morgan, is convinced that we are going to win the match today. This, he has decided, is the upbeat story the cricketing public has been waiting for, and in order to cover it in an appropriately celebratory mood he has issued instructions for his cricket writer to report the day's play from the pool, complete with rum punch and anything else he happens to lay his hands on.

Game on, 173 more runs to win, all wickets intact. Players to positions, please, watch and stay. Andy Caddick has gone up to the Sky television box; the rest of us go to roughly the same places we were in last evening. We hope we will not be able to move all day.

Ath and Alec take up where they left off. If anything, they are even more in control. When Alec stands tall and hits one

134

through mid-wicket, is there a finer sight in cricket? They rotate the strike brilliantly, sharing the bowling, sharing the responsibility and although Lara rings the changes to keep everything alive, the quietness around the Oval tells us we are just getting hold of this one. His juggling of resources is intriguing. Having started with the big two, he switches to spin at one end, Adams and Hoops and then gives Amby and Courtney two spells of one over then two overs each. It was almost as though he was just trying to upset the concentration of the batsmen. At times, they bowled with one slip and a ring of fielders saving singles, and at others he called all his fielders into the catching positions. Is he attacking or defending, or just playing silly buggers to put the boys off their stride. Did it work? On 39, Ath should have been caught by Stuart Williams in the gully, but was badly put down. No theories work when fielders drop catches.

The clouds, thank God, are staying put, and so do Alec, Athers and everyone else until lunch, when we are 122 for no wicket. One hundred and three runs to get now, five sessions, all ten wickets and no sign of Hurricane Curtly. For the second time in a row, the side batting last has to make the highest score of the match to win it and so far, this is when the pitches have played at their easiest. Is this back-to-front cricket or what? If this happens again, perhaps we should stick them in and reverse the batting order. On second thoughts. Me. Philip Tufnell. Opening the batting for England. Against Courtney Walsh and Curtly Ambrose, two of the most fearsome fast bowlers in the world. When the pitch is at its most sporting. With my reputation?

Wake up. Just after lunch, Athers gets a snorter from Walsh which bounces and moves away and he edges it to Williams – 129 for one. Okay. Okay. At least I can get up and stretch my legs now. Caddy returns from the Sky box to ask:

'Dont suppose there's any lunch left, boys?' He's right. Sorry caddy.

Slight jangle on the nerves, but fewer than a hundred left now. It's going to be all right, isn't it? Isn't it?

Well, yes, but … No-one is saying it, of course, but in the back of our minds, maybe in some cases nearer the front, as it happens, we know that Curtly has the ability to win games in seconds.

Now Creeps, who has got a little bit stuck, tries to push for a second run when possibly it isn't necessary, takes on the arm of Kenny Benjamin and after countless television replays, loses – 145 for two.

These things happen. Not to worry. Still only eighty to win.

Only.

Nass goes in to join Alec. Okay now. These boys will do it for us. Half an hour more of Al and we will be there. Come on, Nass, you can play against these blokes. You did it in the first innings last week. Just play as you did.

What did I say? Al gets a ball from Walsh he can do nothing about. 152 for three. Chalks is out there now with Nass and they have one eye on the clouds that seem now to be awaiting instructions from some higher power. Nothing fancy, nice and steady. By now, every run is precious and every four a gift from heaven. So when Nass walks down the track and plants Hoops back over his head one bounce for four, it's almost like we have won the match. Oh, Christ, where did that come from? Nass gets a ball from Hoops that lands and then runs right along the ground into his pads – 168 for four.

Just starting to get a little bit twitchy. Only fifty-seven to get now, but after these two and Jack we are down to the tail and don't their boys know it?

Butch and Chalks play nice and steady, but we do not actually seem to be going anywhere. Suddenly, the rotation of the strike has stopped.

I decide I cannot sit here and watch any more of this. The question is how to make the time pass. Brilliant idea. My dance music compact disc had fourteen songs on it. Fourteen songs at, say, three and three-quarter minutes each makes, er, fifty-two and a half minutes. Right. I go down to the physio's room below, stretch out on the couch and plug in my walkman. I can just about hear the cheers and the wooohs from down here, but by the time the CD is completed, we will have taken the game on by 52 and a half minutes...

So there I am, during the most tense passage of play in the most tense Test match I have ever played in, lying on the physio's couch listening to dance music. Now that's how you get a bad name.

Fantastic. My head is emptied of everything. The music stops and I climb the stairs back to the dressing-room, fifty-two and a half minutes later to discover that during that time we have scored SEVEN RUNS. SEVEN.

The boys are batting well, apparently, but Walsh and Amby are just not giving them anything to hit. And now the rain comes. And those who have been the victims of the Port-of-Spain curse start looking a bit pale.

This is so agonising. The boys go out then come off. Go out again, then come off. Absolutely vital not to lose any more wickets tonight, but we must try and get something on the board. If you stop picking up singles and allow them to bowl at you, they will kill you.

Finally, play is called off. We are 187 for four. Just 38 to get. We are nearly there, lads, nearly there.

Gallows humour, now. ' Cat, it's all set up for you to score the winning runs tomorrow. Hee. Hee. Hee.' NO IT IS NOT.

137

I WILL NOT BE OUT THERE. I WILL NOT BE OUT THERE, GEDDIT?

Sorry, boys. Just getting to me a bit.

Decide to try and get away from the hotel which is full of English supporters who want to talk about the cricket. They mean well, but I'm afraid this is the last thing we want to do.

Out to dinner with Ashley, Caddy, Nass and Butch, who, despite being not out nine overnight facing the biggest day of his Test career tomorrow, is the most relaxed of the lot.

We try to talk about other things to keep our minds off tomorrow. About life, the universe and EastEnders, but it's useless. Although we have banned any discussion about the cricket, now matter how hard we try the thing keeps coming back. The boys are jittery, no doubt, and we all look at Butch for a sign. All he says is 'Good vibes, man. Good vibes.' Talk about cool under pressure. We are choking on our chinese and he is sitting there, completely iced.

Difficulty getting to sleep. Then, in the confines of my four walls, I affect indifference. No point in worrying about it. This time tomorrow it will be over one way or the other. And all that will have happened is that I will be one day older.

I should co-co.

Tuesday 17 February, Third Test, Day 5

England 2nd inns 225–5 (Butcher 24*, Headley 7)
This is it, then. Thirty-eight runs to win, six wickets left. Sounds a doddle, doesn't it? An absolute piece of pie.

I prepare for what may turn out to be my moment of destiny with some scratchy throw-downs in front of the pavilion, and then after this largely irrelevant exercise is completed, once again assume crash position. Look at Chalks and Butch before they go out to bat. They appear unfussed, calm, almost serene. But what is going on inside them?

Those clouds are about, again. Bastards. Just sort of mocking us. 'As if you haven't got enough to worry about' they seem to be saying, 'what with Curtly and Courtney. Just remember, we can mess you up any time we like.'

Just for fun, and as a reminder of their power, they let some out and the start is delayed by rain. Jack is sitting, quietly cursing. If this one is washed out, I do not care to think what he will do. Are we EVER going to get this bloody game finished?

The rain stops, and finally we start about forty minutes late. Settle down to it and we start off all right. Lovely, lovely, some nice running between the wickets and the boys are edging us up there. The 200 comes up and this is a massive psychological boost. Just 25 to get now and we will be there. But they are still bowling so bloody tight.

The little corner of the dressing-room where me and Creeps are watching has become Fag city. I'm reminded of the climax of the movie *Airplane*, when Lloyd Bridges, the bloke trying to talk the pilot down, grows increasingly frantic as the time comes for him to try and land the plane. 'Looks like I picked the wrong day to quit smoking,' he says as the tension mounts. I know how he feels.

Butch is holding it together well (good vibes, man) but they are not bowling bad balls. A typical over: leave, leave, play-and-miss, block, block (look for a single, no single), block. And in the dressing-room we are quietly dying. Gus and I take a quick look at each other. Neither of us speaks. No words are necessary, because we know exactly what the other is thinking ... No, it won't come to that. We'll be all right.

Big blow. Chalks is out, caught by the keeper off Amby. Sod it. Not now. Not now.

Twenty-four to get, Butch and Jack at the wicket. Now

Jack, scuttling and squeezing, helps Butch cut the target even further. We are scoring the runs off like a man in his prison cell counting the days. And it is sooo quiet.

The tension and the silence are broken momentarily when Jack goes forward to play at one and somehow loses his glove in the process. We crowd around the telly to see what has happened and Creeps says: 'Hold on, Jack's hand has come off.' The laughter is hysterical, in the true sense of the word. We are clutching, I can tell you. AND THEN JACK IS OUT and the laughter stops. We are 213, still twelve to get and we are now six wickets down, with Caddy, Deano, Gus AND THEN ME.

As Caddy goes in, Gus starts to get himself prepared. The man is struggling. He starts scrambling around for his gear and putting it on in a not very controlled manner. I'm in my shorts and I try to help, but the space is cramped and he gets both feet stuck in one trouser leg and he's trying to get his shirt on and he can't find the right arm-hole and he's searching for his pads and he can't find them and he can't find his boots and he's shouting 'Where's my boots?' and I'm shouting 'Calm down, calm down, we'll find your ...' and CADDY IS OUT FIRST BALL...

'Sod your boots, Fraze,' I say, 'WHERE ARE MINE?'. Needless to say my kit is absolutely everywhere. Looks like I picked the wrong day to give up sniffing glue.

In the midst of this terrifying panic Deano strolls out, seemingly without a care. We are praying now for the ghost of the legendary George to help us out. With only Gus and me left, where are you George, when we need you? Deano and Butch scrape six runs together and then it is lunch. At a time like this. Lunch.

Butch comes into the dressing-room, slams down his bat and asks: 'Is there any f***ing chance of a half-volley or a long-hop? I have been out there for an hour and a half and I ain't had one sodding ball to hit.'

Deano, who invariably has a unique perspective on these things, decides that this is the time to lie down and have a nap. He takes his pads off, settles down in the corner of the dressing-room and, within moments, is fast asleep. Gus and I aren't hungry, in fact I'm feeling a little queasy. So we potter about the room trying not to wake Deano up. Athers pokes his head around the door, sees Gus and me looking white as sheets, quivering and shaking and enquires: 'All right, boys?' To which neither of us has uttered a word. He says: 'Don't worry. It'll be over soon.' Looks like I picked the wrong day to give up amphetamines.

Just before Dean and Butch go out again, Al chirps up: 'I had a dream last night, Cat.'

'Oh, yes.' I say, 'What was that, then?'

'I dreamed that you went out with four to win.'

By this time everyone is cocking an ear.

'What happened?' I ask.

'I don't know. I woke up.'

Gus is sitting there almost in a trance. His face is completely devoid of expression but his legs are shaking. There is a pain in this desire to win. It really, really hurts.

Everyone is now winding me up. Go on, Cat, you're going to do it. It's going to be up to you. And I'm pleading: 'NO. NO. NO.' In fact I start to devise my plan for what to do if I have to go out there. I decide that if it comes to it, I'm going to have a swipe.

Fully padded up, with my bowling spikes on, for some reason I also decide to watch what is left of the proceedings from the toilet. From my vantage point I watch the telly in a small side mirror. This means that everything I see is back to front, adding a certain surreal touch. Left-arm over Curtly

141

bowls to right-handed Butch and left-handed Deano. And then Dean plays the greatest shot of all time, against Courtney. I watch his drive go past Jimmy Adams at short leg and then the camera pans back and we all realise that THERE IS NO MID-ON. I jump up from the loo seat, taking no account of the fact that the floor is tiled. Half-way to my feet I start to slip and slide and skate like Bambi on ice. I'm flapping about trying to regain my balance but, from somewhere I can hear myself shouting at the top of my voice 'RUN. RUN ... RUN...'

Now calm down. Butch takes a single and there are two runs to win the match.

Next over, Amby to Butch. He bowls a bloody no-ball. Scores level. Come on. Come on. Next ball nothing ... and then the most beautiful extra in England's Test history. Amby bowls one right across Butch and down the leg side, David Williams dives full stretch and just parries the ball and everyone screams: 'RRRRRUUUUUUUUUUUUNNNN...'

They do. That's it. It's over. Pandemonium. It's been like walking a tightrope covered in broken glass but WE HAVE WON THE TEST MATCH.

Suddenly realise I have not taken a breath for the best part of two days.

The over-riding feeling is relief; relief that we have won, relief that after last week we have proved that we are not chokers, relief that we are not 2–0 down, relief that we do not have to play this match one second longer.

Everywhere you look people are grabbing hold of each other. And then, after the initial surge of elation, a spot of quiet, almost as though we are wondering what happens now. Supermac comes in to say well done, Pack tries to but the moment he gets through the door he is covered in beer and champagne.

People sometimes say that you shouldn't get too carried away with this stuff. In my day it was shake hands, well played and see you in the bar afterwards. Only a game? It's only a game when you lose.

A few of their boys come into our dressing room. Jimmy Adams says he has never played in a Test match anywhere near anything like it. They are all feeling the emotion of what has just taken place. After all, had they won it the series would more or less have been theirs. Courtney comes in and says he bowled only one bad ball in 37 overs, the one Deano hit for three. And he isn't joking.

The presentation happens, man-of-the-match for Gus etc. Slightly different feeling from last week. Shattered, but this time elated too.

We get back to the hotel and some silly stuff in the pool. Everyone gets dumped in, even Supermac, with Beefy in the thick of it as usual. Many glasses of wine, then repair to Botham's for a glass or two more. Lara is holding a party at his house on the hill overlooking the Savannah and we are all invited. Lara spends most of the evening with his arm round a very, very drunk Athers. Back to the Pelican for more with the Barmy Army, most of whom, like us, are now categorically smashed. Not quite sure how I got back to my room.

Wednesday 18 February

I am really most awfully sorry, but I have absolutely no idea whatsoever about what happened today.

Strange rumours are circulating to the effect that the captain may be turning into an alcoholic. These stem from the fact that after every Test match so far on this tour (two and a bit, to be precise), win, lose or draw, Ath has gone out and got himself absolutely shedded to release the tension. And on his trips he has invariably been accompanied by a coterie of minders – Gus, Nass and Ash among the regulars – whose job it has been to get him safely back to his pit at the end of the evening. Anyone got the number for AA?

CHAPTER EIGHT

Curtly and Courtney and the bomb squad

Thursday 19, February. Trinidad to Georgetown, Guyana

The mists are clearing slowly. Today we fly to Guyana. Guyana may be Guyana, but at least we are getting away from those flaming drums. No offence. Whilst performing the obligatories in trap one at the airport and gazing at the toilet door, as one does, I notice three more explanations for the initials BWIA, to go along with those previously mentioned. They are: 'Britain's Worst Investment Anywhere', 'Better Walk If Able' and, my personal favourite, 'But Will It Arrive?'. No offence, again.

Haven't particularly been looking forward to getting to Georgetown. Although the violence and bombs etc that put the Test here in jeopardy seem to have subsided, memories of my visit here four years ago are not very pleasant. To put it mildly, we felt that the whole place needed a lick of paint then and the hotel, the Pegasus, especially. Two to a small room last time round, the smell of the damp was occasionally overpowering. In fact, thumbing through the local *Stabroek News* (owned, incidentally, by the father of Athers' Guyanese girlfriend, Isabelle De Caires) I read that the President, Janet Jagan, has called for a 'massive clean-up exercise for Georgetown', saying that both the government and the council recognise that the city is in a deplorable state.

The President called 'for neighbourhood brigades to dispose of piled up garbage, for citizens to desist from throwing rubbish on the streets and to ensure that we don't hang our heads in shame for not cleaning up the environment.'

Guyana is currently also in the grip of the effects of El Nino. Not wet, this time, but dry. The first rainy season, months back, passed without any and the paddy fields are cracked and parched, the livestock dying of lack of food and water and a campaign has been launched to save the manatees in the local zoo. These sea cows live in a muddy pond at Georgetown Zoo which is all but dried up.

The journey into Georgetown from the airport along the banks of the Demerara River is not instructive. Can't see many changes here, except that the road has finally been finished. But the trip does take us past the Banks's brewery, located at the aptly named Thirst Park. Which reminds me. Hold it. Hold it.

To be fair, we are all a tad too knackered for that kind of behaviour at the moment, but arrival at the hotel brings a nice surprise, and not only for Athers – whose girlfriend Izzy is here to greet him. It has been brightened up considerably, the rooms are all okay and refurbished and everyone appears incredibly pleased to see us.

Ned's Bar has gone, where eight years ago Wayne 'Ned' Larkins made alcohol history on one of the rain-sodden days of the washed-out Test by sitting on the same corner stool from opening to closing time, downing bottles of Banks beer and packets of B & H and rising only, from time to time, for the necessary siphoning. Also gone are the two fantastically exotic parrots that used to live in the gardens, the squawking,

146

amorous advances towards Robin Smith of one nearly causing our middle-order batsman to lose an eye.

The rooms all have sea views, but this is not the turquoise shimmery Caribbean stuff, rather, as we are on the northern coast of South America, the muddy brown Atlantic. There is a beach, but it is definitely no go and you would swim here only avoid drowning.

It's now starting to hit me that I am completely shattered. Back-to-back Tests in the space of thirteen days, and with such tension and pressure all the time, have taken their toll. I have never been involved in a cricketing experience like it. During two Test matches squeezed into a little over ten days absolutely every ball meant something. My nails are bitten to the quick and I have been getting throgh about a tousand fags per day. And when you were stuck in the middle of it all, you felt like it was never, ever going to end.

The game against Guyana is due to start on Saturday. To be honest – and I would never say this to the management – I wouldn't mind having it off, as they say.

Friday 20 February

As the day goes on the word grows stronger that Crofty and I are both going to play tomorrow and then at the team meeting in the evening this is confirmed.

On one level I am glad as this means we may be paired for the Test match. I enjoy bowling with another spinner at the other end, as I did with Embers at Middlesex for years. It just takes the pressure off a little if you are not the only spinner in the side and if two of you are operating in tandem that means the game is being played at a spinner's pace. It's a little too simplistic to suggest that, working in tandem, spinners can crack a batsman with the old one-two or anything like that, but some of the most successful in history have hunted in pairs just like pacemen. In fact, whether the Bourda Oval is going to be a raging bunsen burner or not I personally think that if you can play two spinners and there aren't compelling factors against doing so, a side is better balanced if you do. Not for me to reason why, though.

On another level, the fact that both of us are going to play at the Everest ground tomorrow does raise the possibility that a shoot-out is being lined up between us in case they decide that only one of us plays in the Test match. In the past I have been accused of not reacting well to the pressure of competition for places. To be fair, I'm not certain I'm the best at it either.

Yes, I have bowled to instructions and to the plan that the majority have favoured. Yes, some umpiring decisions haven't gone my way and yes, chances have gone begging. But whatever the reasons I have not taken the wickets I should have done.

Neither Robbo or I will go into the game hoping the other does badly. We are good mates, we think the same way about most aspects of the game and as far as our craft is concerned we both like to be mean and yet to attack at the same time. In Zimbabwe and New Zealand last year we took 32 wickets together in the five Tests played and started to build a proper partnership and that sort of thing is never given enough credence. If only one spinner is picked for the Test and it isn't me, I'll say best of luck, and I will really mean it. But just somewhere at the back of the mind, is there a slight feeling of every man for himself?

What will not help me either way is that I am dog tired. (Or should that be cat-tired?)

Whilst thinking about all of the above, forget that Ramps is at last going to get a chance. He has been busting a gut to play and when laid low by the lurgy for the last Test in

Trinidad he might have thought that someone was trying to tell him something. But he's here and he'll be having a go. Playing in the land where his dad was born as well. Mills and Boon are on stand-by for the next fortnight.

Saturday 21 February Guyana v England

Got out the wrong side this morning. Supermac's decree that we all have our own hotel rooms (imposed after he saw us playing sardines in Harare last winter) is all well and good, and they have obviously smartened this place up no end, but most of the lads are in rooms with twin beds. As one of these is barely wide enough for Kate Moss to lie down sideways (hmm, there's a thought. Sorry Lisa. Rolling pin on head), the new arrangements are slightly beside the point. I have not slept well and I am in a shit mood.

Try to clear my head with an early walk along the sea wall at the back of the hotel, during which I pass by the Everest ground on the land side and a hideously dead dog on the beach. Rigor Mortis has set in and the poor sod is bloated and stinks. I am almost sick with the stench.

When we get to the ground all I can think of and pray for is that Athers wins the toss so that I can put my feet up for a day. So when he calls incorrectly and Chanderpaul, their captain, asks us to bowl first into a cross-gale, there follows a severe test of my mental attitude.

Not very proud to report that I fail with flying colours.

Now I hope people understand that on tour, and especially on a tour like this when for two weeks I feel like I've had my head in a vice, there comes a time when the last thing you want to be doing is playing a game of cricket. This will sound like blasphemy to all those who believe that representing England under any circumstances is the nearest you can get to being waved through by St. Peter, and I assure you that there is nothing like walking out to play in a Test match; I do understand why the management want me to play, and I know how lucky I am to be doing this for a living at all, etc., BUT after almost seven weeks on tour I actually wouldn't have minded a few days R & R. You simply cannot keep up the same level of intensity all the time or you will eventually just blow your brains out.

The pitch lives up to advance billing and turns square from early on. Crofty gets among them and has a long stint, interrupted by lunch and tea only, taking six for 50. He bowls really well. Athers obviously has taken the hint about my state of mind and health and gives me enough overs to find a rhythm but not too many. He can see that I am finding it terribly hard to get 100 per cent out of myself. I take one wicket. The only lightish moment comes when I have a bowl at their opener Clayton Lambert. He has a fantastic record in domestic cricket and is being touted locally for a Test recall. We do not take this all that seriously as he is as old as Noah and when he bats he appears to take guard facing extra cover, but we do know he is capable of smashing it everywhere. This is the first time I have bowled at him since he helped kick-start my Test career back in 1991. Final Test of the summer series versus West Indies at The Oval, Tufnell's debut. We bat first and score 419 (Tufnell 2). *Wisden* recalls: 'The third day belonged to Tufnell ... From 158 for three, West Indies declined rapidly to 176 all out as Tufnell spun the ball generously in a devastating spell of six for 4 in 33 deliveries either side of lunch. It has to be said, though, that a rash of reckless strokes contributed to this collapse, which began when Lambert miscued Tufnell's first ball of the day to cover, ' and that is, of course, only the second time I have ever read that particular passage to myself. 'Remember The Oval, cat' comes the call and

Clayton obviously does as he proceeds to block the shit out of it.

But the worst moment comes when one of their batsmen, don't ask which, skies a sweep off Crofty towards me in the deep. It's gone into bloody orbit and it's swirling in the bloody gale and I get absolutely bloody nowhere near it. I must look a right pillock and I don't help myself by having a quiet kick at the ground in response. Anyone observing my performance might have felt I was sulking a bit. To be honest, I probably was. Situation eased by the fact that we skittle them for 135 for nine, then situation not helped when their last pair go and put on nearly fifty which just about pisses me off completely.

Cheered up somewhat when informed of the following prank. Stephen Bull, our latest recruit from the world of sports psychology has arrived and throughout the day has been, very publicly, having his ear bent by Caddy on the boundary right next to the press tent. Some mischief-maker among the hacks, meanwhile, has persuaded one of his more experienced colleagues that Bull has graduated to this role following several successful seasons as centre-forward for Wolverhampton Wanderers. The victim resolves to seek an interview with Bully over his remarkable career-change.

Sunday 22 February

Today is the 28th anniversary of the formation of the Republic Of Guyana. Happy anniversary, Guyana. In the Chronicle, the poet Pamela Dolly Hytmiah has penned these words for the occasion.

Rise, Guyana, rise:
Rise Guyana, rise
To the challenges before your eyes

151

Climb to new heights sublime
Leave the past behind
You are not downtrodden,
sodden, or forgotten
But begotten and chosen to be free
And to fulfil your destiny

Dance Guyana, dance
Forget your grievance
Put away your confusion
And join in the celebration ...
... One People, One nation, One Destiny
Land of the brave and the free
With God's help we shall certainly
Cover new territory.

Leap Guyana, leap
Wake up from your sleep
This is no time to weep
This is a time to reap
Let yourselves go
And move with the flow
Join your hearts as one
And pray for our nation

Yes, Guyana, yes
We can accomplish the task
There's nothing too great or too small
That you cannot conquer at all
You are destined to be great
Strive to achieve your fate
With one heart let us unite
Together we shall win the fight.

And I really don't think there is anything I can usefully add to that.

Ramps is clearly inspired by the anniversary and digs us out of the shloot. 56 for three when he goes in, all three wickets to their left-arm spinner Neil McGarrell, which makes me feel ten times better, of course, then 60 for four when Athers is caught at the wicket of the quickish Reon King (lightning, I seem to recall, or is he thunder?), Ramps bats for the rest of the day, 265 minutes, making 68 not out and with Smokes (36) and Crofty (25 not out) takes us past their total.

Really, really pleased for Ramps. The fact that he has scored runs is no surprise to me as I know how good he is. But I did wonder earlier on in the tour is he was going to be able to hold himself together and keep his focus. He is a very intense character, who as he admits, suffered in his early years from an acute desire to get there yesterday. I know how he has suffered knockback after knockback, but I know how good he is and I am a big fan. He must be given a chance in the Test now, surely. Can he take it this time?

Chat with him in the evening and he is chuffed. He knows that this might have been his last opportunity. Funny how things go, though. Creeps, the one whose place is probably under most threat, played onto his stumps against McGarrell (I'm sorry but I just cannot get the words 'book him, Danno' out of my head) while Ramps survived what they call a 'confident appeal' for a catch behind when he was only three. By such margins etc.

Monday 23 February

Talking of which, completely terrible news today from Dhaka, where a former Test player, Raman Lamba, has died from head injuries sustained while fielding in a club match.

Lamba, who played four times for India, and, somewhat bizarrely, four times for Ireland, was fielding at short leg without a helmet when he was hit on the forehead. He was able to walk back to the dressing room where he vomited and was then rushed to a clinic, then hospital. His condition deteriorated and he was placed on a life support system. It was finally switched off eight hours after he had been pronounced clinically dead. He was 38. Makes you think about all the times those bastards made you field at short leg in a school or club match with some nutter swinging from the hip against less than metronomic accuracy.

Back to Everest where young McGarrell finishes with seven for 71 (d-d-d-da ... daa-daa,). Some local business-man, known as 'Uncle Joe' Hilliare is so chuffed that McGarrell has made his career-best that he presents him with a cheque for 20,000 Guyanese dollars, approx. £85. This is about as exciting as the game looks like becoming. We get a lead and the match seems to be going nowhere when Lambert and Nicholas de Groot are busy rattling up 71 or the first wicket. Then, suddenly, they lose all ten wickets for 60 runs, five to Crofty and, thank God, five to me. I bowled all right, actually, but I have to say that they did not bat as though their lives depended on it. They're all out for 131 and we have to get 77 in fifteen overs. Twelve are taken from the first over but they then get the message and start bowling wide of the leg stump making it impossible to play shots, very reminiscent of the first Test against Zim in Bulawayo last winter. We lose three wickets in quick succession, give up the chase and settle for and early finish and some net practice in the middle.

At least I ended the match in better frame of mind than when I started. The second innings five for 42 and the way Crofty and I bowled together has eased my concerns over

154

playing in the next Test. Feeling adventurous I try out an item on the menu in a nearby restaurant I have not seen before. Can't recall the name exactly ... Marau. Marra, Mara, something like that ... but I am informed by the waiter that it tastes like chicken. Indeed it does. Quite delicious. One to watch for.

Tuesday 24 February

Rest day. Visit the Georgetown Zoo to see the endangered Manatee and the wonderful eagles. Then I see last night's mystery dinner item in the flesh. On the name plate is written the latin name, *Dolichotis patagonum*, then Mara, it's common-use name, and a description reading: 'a hare-like South American rodent'. Realisation slowly dawns that I have partaken of rat. A big, fat, hairy rat with whiskers. And I ate it all up. Resolve to be not quite so adventurous in future.

Rest day in Guyana. Surely a not-to-be-missed opportunity for us all to toddle off to see one of the great sights, the Kaiteur Falls, a million feet higher than Niagara etc. and spectacular in the extreme. Four years ago we travelled there and it was more than worth the trip. One photograph of the skipper leaning over the edge still does my head in every time I see it. The trouble is that this time we are all completely knackered. This probably won't go down too well with the get-out-and-see-it-all school of thought, but no-one, but no-one can be arsed to make the trip. Am I getting blase? I don't think so. In any case I'm too tired to tell. Sleep.

Wednesday 25 February

Sleep. Potter around, Sleep. Potter around. Hear that Hoops may be in trouble with the West Indies board because he refused to play for Guyana in the match against us. Concerned with their low scores in the Test series so far (apart from the 282 for seven to win the second Test in Port-of-Spain, they have made 191, 159 and 210) their coach Malcolm Marshall and manager Clive Lloyd had issued a directive that all their batsmen should play for their territories in the matches between Tests. Whereas Chanderpaul played against us, Lara played for Trinidad and Tobago against Jamaica for whom Jimmy Adams made 203 not out and Sherwin Campbell played for Barbados against Windward Islands, Hoops was the only one who had a match to play in and didn't. He stayed in Trinidad where he is moving house from Guyana and 'phoned the Guyana Board late last Tuesday to tell them he wasn't coming. No explanation. Nothing.

Even the Windies boys say that 'cool Carl' is a law unto himself. Evidently the Board is still waiting for an explanation from him for his strange behaviour at the Hong Kong international six-a-side tournament last September. Although appointed captain of the team, he failed to select himself for a single match and never once made it onto the field. A letter in the *Stabroek News* asks: 'Is Carl Hooper a true Guyanese?' Some are saying that the Board might even drop him from the Test squad for failing to play against us. Pull the other one. It has bells on it.

Thursday 26 February

More close observation of the Test pitch at Bourda by both sides and it seems that West Indies are also convinced that the pitch will take spin. El Nino has done it's work here and the pitch is bare and very dry. So much so that the Windies have picked only four fast bowlers in their squad as opposed to the customary six. And they have included a specialist leg-spinner, the almost unpronounceable Ramnarine who made such an impression at Guaracara Park the other week. Those for whom red leather–yellow leather no longer provides a serious challenge should try him after a couple of pints. There would appear to be little point in the Trinidad and Tobago spinner turning up if he is not going to play. Hoops has also been included in their squad, surprise, surprise, although their chairman of selectors Wes Hall is clearly not best pleased. 'I consider it totally unacceptable that a member of the team, and the vice-captain at that, should not abide by the wishes of the coach. It is a flagrant dereliction of duty and a breach of authority.' he says. He's still playing though, isn't he?

Later in the day comes our team meeting. Pick up vibes that both Crofty and me are going to play but nothing definite. They will make the final pick before kick-off tomorrow. Now comes one of the rituals of the tour, the show put on by the first-time tourists for the benefit of everyone else. Murgatroyd is very impressive as the master of ceremonies while Dean Headley looks incredibly fanciable in a two-piece, in a sort of Grace Jonesish way. In fact, PHhwwooar.

What *am* I saying?

The highlight, all that *amore* stuff apart, is Smokes' impersonation of our avuncular tour manager Bob Bennett in the mastermind chair. Questions include: 'What would you do if the luggage didn't turn up? Would you a) Flap about a bit. b) Say 'it's nothing to do with me. Ask the scorer.' c) Go and have a cup of tea?' All very tongue-in-cheek, of course…

Levity apart, we know how important tomorrow's match is. If we want to win the series we must try and get to Barbados for the back-to-back final Tests at least on level terms. If we are 2–1 up with two to play, Bingo. If we are 2–1 down...

Friday 27 February, Fourth Test, Bourda Oval, Day 1

Close of play: West Indies 1st inns 271–3 (Chanderpaul 100*, Hooper 36*)

In the morning paper appears a slightly alarming reminder of the political unrest that at one stage threatened our visit here. Protesters yesterday stoned the car of the President, Janet Jagan outside the parliament building. No-one was hurt and the President herself was unharmed, but the tension that surrounded the elections is still just under the surface. In fact people fear that once we are out of the way and gone things may flare up again. Quite glad I won't be around to find out. But incidents like this do just get you wobbling a bit.

Once at the ground all thoughts are back to the cricket, though.

There are no two ways about it. From the look of the bald top, there is only going to be one day to bat on this pitch and that day is today. After that, God knows what is going to happen to it.

Picking two spinners and only two seamers isn't exactly a gamble but it will suit us best to win the toss, bat first then bowl at them last on a crumbling surface.

In order to be able to do that, of course, we must first win the toss.

We lose the toss.

What was that about two seamers and two spinners? After two overs Deano is warned for the second time by umpire Steve Bucknor for running on the pitch, which is about the most ridiculous thing I have ever seen on a cricket field. Once more and the umpire will automatically instruct

158

Athers not to bowl him again in the innings and then our pace bowling department will consist of Gus and whatever Mark Butcher can muster.

After the second warning Athers goes up to Deano and tells him: 'For Christ's sake keep off the effing pitch.' But although Bucknor told him he has encroached the danger area, on the line of the stumps and on a seamer's length, three times, Dean insists that he has hardly been near it. And his version of events is later supported by those watching television close-ups of the action, including allegedly, the match referee Barry Jarman.

Kind of strange that Deano has not been warned for this at all in the series until now, when he is one of only two seamers and under huge pressure to perform. The last thing he needs in the circumstances is to start worrying about where his feet are landing, but the last thing we need is for him to be forced out of the attack.

Fortunately the crisis passes and Deano and Gus strike to remove both openers cheaply at 38 for two. This brings Lara and Chanderpaul together. Keep the pressure on now. One more strike and we could be through. Then, Chanderpaul on nine, push-drives at Gus and the ball goes quick and low but not impossibly so towards Alec at second slip ... and down. Difficult chance, but we all know that in the circumstances, after having lost the toss on a pitch that will merely get worse we must grab everything that comes our way. How costly will this miss turn out to be?

How costly? Very, to be precise. Chanderpaul and Lara now put on put on 159 for the third wicket. The pitch is good for batting and the boundaries small and the outfield quick. Made for batting, in fact, and they do so well, without taking risks and positively. For the first time in the series Lara looks and is in ominous form. Not merely does he unleash his powerhouse shots but, and for me this is the key to telling he is in nick. he starts to play the field. Balls from seam bowlers that they feel might induce an edge are glided and guided around and gaps found at will. Against two slips, a gully and third man he steers the ball just wide enough of second slip and fine enough of third man to go all the way to the line. Magnificent to watch except if you are the poor bowler who thinks he has produced a jaffa, maybe even for them as well. Quiet please, genius at work.

Of course the crowd is absolutely loving this. Chanderpaul, local hero, captain of Guyana, who made his Test debut here against us four years ago, is batting excellently as well. Crofty gets Lara somewhat out of the blue, with a good piece of bowling. He gives the ball a bit more air and Lara drives it to Chalks at deep extra cover, out for 93. Hoops strides in to accompany Chanderpaul, so there are now two Guyanese at the wicket in front of the most fervent supporters in the entire West Indies region.

The stage is set for Chanderpaul as he closes in on his second Test hundred. No Guyanese has made one here since Clive Lloyd made 178 against Australia in 1973.

And then, in the last but one over of the day, it happens. Chanderpaul flicks me through extra cover comes back for the second run to complete the hundred and the ground is swamped.

By this time the pitch is already starting to disintegrate, but the celebrations of the crowd just speed up the process. Chanderpaul does his best to shoo the spectators off the pitch but he has no chance. Hundreds of them come charging on, with very little or no effort made to stop them by police or stewards as far as we can see, and they all seem to be making straight for the track. Standing at one end and looking down the pitch I can see a rasta wining and grinding

160

on a good length in his big heavy boots, while a few of the locals getting somewhat over-excited, pass on a few words of advice. 'Tufnell, you shit, man. Chanderpaul giving you licks', the usual. There's not a lot we can do except sit there and wait for the surge to subside.

There's not a lot we can do except sit there and wait for the surge to subside. I don't think the spectators are deliberately trying to rough up the pitch but, whether they are or not, that is the effect of their actions. What really gets to us is that there is virtually no attempt whatsoever by the authorities to stop them. All over the Caribbean throughout the tour the West Indies Board have taken out advertisements in the local papers warning that spectators should not run on the pitch. No-one objects in the slightest to enthusiasm and exuberance – thank God people can still get so carried away and passionate about Test cricket – but when the game itself is affected by the actions of the crowd then the line has been overstepped.

We are aware enough as it is that the pitch is going to 'go', but this business at the end of a day when they have put a score on the door, does little to cheer us up.

The sight of Chanderpaul standing there on the pitch patting down the surface surrounded by about thirty people whose boots are doing more and more damage is quite comical. And then there is the aspect of player safety. Crofty got collared by one bloke and a few started to have a go at me. You have to turn the other cheek, but when you've been getting it in the ear from the boundary edge all through a very long, very hot day it is quite difficult not to think about an eye for an eye. Let's just say you cannot imagine this sort of thing happening at HQ.

We finish up then troop off and collapse in the dressing room. After two Test matches in Trinidad when the door to the dressing room revolved, spending a whole day out in that red hot heat was a reminder of what touring out here is normally like. Bloody hard work.

We think we have hung in and scrapped well. Although they are 271 for three, after a day's batting on a good pitch with a lightning outfield and small boundaries, they are not out of sight. BUT, there is no doubt that, at one end, the rough is opening up and a variety of different sized and shaped holes are starting to appear. What we must do is make sure Chanderpaul and Hooper don't take the game away tomorrow morning.

Sitting round the pool that evening it is hard to avoid the feeling that the toss has gone their way and that this Test match is going to be extremely hard to save let alone win. Not too much good humour as we scoff a selection of pizzas and knock back a few Banks's. We have worked so hard all tour. If we do lose now the feeling that the result has probably been decided by the toss of a coin will be no comfort whatsoever.

Saturday 28 February, Fourth Test, Day 2

Close of play: West indies 1st innings 352 all out; England 1st innings 87 for 6 (Ramprakash 13 * not out. Croft 5 * not out.
Perturbing beginning to the day. Just before the start of play we are all sitting around the dressing room getting ready to go out when four blokes march in and announce they are the bomb disposal squad.

'Sorry?'.

'We have received a telephone call warning that there is a bomb in the England dressing room. Please remain calm while we carry out a search.'

Which they proceed to do, lifting up paper cups and old socks and peering underneath. This fine-toothcomb treatment lasts all of a minute-and-a-half during which time the members of the bomb disposal squad give the impression they are late for a previous engagement. Finally, and obviously not a moment too soon as far as they are concerned, they take their leave with the following instructions: 'If you see anything that looks like a bomb, please telephone immediately.' After they have scuttled off we realise that they have failed to leave their number.

Later, almost as an after-thought, one of them returns and instructs us to evacuate. The team does so by going onto the field to start the match, the other lads walk at a fair pace around the outfield to sit by the sightscreen and wait for the all-clear. The other occupants of the beautiful old wooden pavilion, namely the members of the Georgetown CC, do not move. We discover later that they were all blissfully unaware of proceedings. It turns out to be a crank caller, and finally, after about half an hour the lads next to the sightscreen troop back in, if a tad gingerly. Interestingly, one or two seem to think they would be of more use to the team staying put and studying the Windies batsmen from behind the arm.

Perhaps this brush with danger has galvanised us . Whatever, we come out very strong and skittle them for 352, taking their last seven wickets for 54. Crofty and I bowl well in tandem, sharing six in all. Nice to bowl together at last. We have kept the screws on them and done the job. AND at last I get an lbw decision bowling over the wicket against a left-hander (Jimmy Adams) playing no shot. Darrell Hair, the Aussie umpire gives it and, although you might think me slightly biased, more power to him; he saw the line of the ball, knew that the bat was jammed behind the front pad and that Jimmy was making no attempt to play a shot, he believed that the ball was going to hit the stumps so he gave it out. Simple. So what about the thirty or forty appeals I had in Trinidad from more-or-less exactly the same deliveries played in more-or-less exactly the same manner in more-or-less exactly the same circumstances? Were NONE of them out? Was not one of those balls going to hit the sticks? The fact is that if umpires do not give more of those decisions in favour of the bowlers then what they will be saying is that, from over the wicket it is impossible for me to bowl balls that are going to hit the stumps. If so, all left-arm spinners may as well pack up the game.

I got quite fed up with it in Trinidad. One of the worst incidents took place in the second Test when I went up for a big appeal against one of their left-handers, Chanderpaul I think. I turned to the umpire for his response to see him peering down at his ball-counter. You might not think it is out, old boy, but at least do me the courtesy of having a look before making up your mind.

Enough of this. I am beginning to sound bitter and twisted. Which, of course, I am.

On a positive note, rattling through them in this way does emphasise again that we are competing. On a slightly less positive note it does also suggest that the pitch is starting to behave in exactly the way we thought it would. And now, they cash in. By the close we are reduced to 87 for six, 265 behind and, from the top end on a seamer's length there is a hole the size of a drinks tray.

We knew that batting would be difficult but this was the same old story, really. Their bowlers had been sitting around for a day and a half with their feet up, watching the pitch deteriorating and biding their time and eyeing their prey like lions in the long grass.

Now they have run in strong, a couple of balls have done

funny things and they are away. Of course, batsmen are supposed to put the previous ball out of their heads and concentrate on playing their natural game – each ball on its merits etc. – and I may have a slightly, er, different approach to these things, but if I am going out to bat to face Courtney and Curtly with their knees hitting their chins, looking down at the pitch and seeing an omelette where solid ground should be would not fill me with the greatest confidence.

To be fair to Walsh and Ambrose they do have a habit of hitting the cracks more often than not. What you might call ability. And when two world class pace bowlers continually find the right spot things are going to happen. It's pretty relentless.

We start badly when Ath is out for a duck to Amby at 1 for one – this is, apparently the thirteenth time Curtly has got him out in Test cricket. Then Courtney, in his 100th Test, bowls like no 35-year-old in his 100th Test has any right to. Unnervingly quick, he manages to cut the ball both ways off the seam and he gets Alec and later Nasser. Meanwhile Amby is bowling like God almighty.

Lara probably didn't need to tell his veteran fast bowlers but this is such a critical phase of the match. They have won the toss and got the score. If they run through us now, the match is theirs and no matter how we have outplayed them until now, maybe the series as well. They STEAM in. Really fast, giving the batsman absolutely nothing to play and beating the bat time after time.

In the middle of all this, at 65 for four, out walks Ramps to resume his Test career. Soon afterwards he is the last recognised batsman, Ramnarine, the leggie having disposed of Chalks and Jack. What is going through Ramps's mind?

Sunday 1 March, Fourth Test, Day 3.

Close of play: England 1st innings 170 all out; West Indies 2nd innings 127 for 9. (Bishop 2*, Walsh 0)

What I do notice from chatting to him last night and watching Ramps again this morning is how calm and relaxed he is. His attitude is this: I've burned myself up over failing too many times before. What is the worst that can happen? I will fail again. I've done that and I'm still standing. So why worry. Go out and enjoy the thing.

He is possibly helped somewhat by Lara's strange decision to keep Amby out of the attack for the entire pre-lunch session. Reasons? Very difficult to answer. Is Lara so confident that we will not reach the follow-on target that he has decided to keep Curtly back for our second innings? And how about this apparently loony suggestion doing the rounds? After what has been produced in Jamaica and Trinidad, the West Indies Board wants to ensure England make a decent score here to avoid any more controversy. Keep taking the tablets.

Whatever Lara's motives, Ramps and Crofty are not complaining. They take us past the hundred and ever nearer to the target of 153 to ensure they must bat again. The slightly unreal atmosphere of the morning session is emphasised when a mangy-looking mongrel, possibly related to the thing I saw on the beach the other day, strolls nonchalantly onto the pitch then proceeds to complete a massive evacuation of the bowel. Clearly, he's not buying Lara' s tactics either.

Up in the stand behind the bowler's arm at the top end Mick Jagger is present, as is Eddy Grant. The legend Jagger is staying at the Hotel, a fact that cannot have escaped the attention of Mark Butcher as he has started to walk up and down the corridors singing VERY LOUDLY.

Ramps bats on and on, collecting where he can, but , after Crofty is out, we collapse. 139 for seven, well batted Robbo, then 139 for eight, bad luck Deano and 140 for nine, well tried Gus and oh my God I am in, with thirteen still required to avoid the follow-on.

A bit of a bonus that I am going out to face Ramnarine and Carl Hooper, but instead of having a slog at them before the quicks return, my game plan is to try and hang around for Ramps to take us to the target. Great moments for Ramps, now. Ten minutes after lunch from successive balls, he first completes his third Test fifty and then scores the runs to take us past the follow-on figure. HUGE respect. And then the fun really starts. Lara is off the field getting attention to a split fingernail and Hoops takes over. He has clearly had enough off all this and immediately brings back Courtney and Curtly at which, of course, my heart sinks.

Curtly decides he is going to bowl around the wicket and directs all six balls at my head. I manage to fend them off then Courtney comes around the wicket and bowls five at my head and one yorker, which was nice of him. At this point, Ramps, who has been standing there pissing himself, relieves me with the words: 'all right cat. I think it might be time to play a few shots.

I have been out there seemingly for weeks but so far have yet to trouble the scorers. Now's my chance to make them pay. Next time I get up to Walsh's end, he bowls me a bouncer. Some reflex nerve in my body lashes out and I try and have a hook. This is not a success. The shot comes out all wrong and I end up looking as though I'm casting a line. The top edge sends the ball sailing up in the air over the wicket-keeper's head and I give it away, convinced that one of the slips is bound to come around and clean it up.

While the ball spirals into the stratosphere Ramps calls me through for a run so I wander down the other end then decide to just keep going towards the pavilion. I'm obviously disappointed to be out but at least we have done the job and saved the follow-on, so let's get out of here because it is dangerous.

Now, unbeknown to me two things have happened. First the fielder, Lara, has dropped the ball which is rolling safely towards the open spaces near the boundary, and secondly the umpire is standing there with his arm outstretched to signify a no-ball. So when I look up at the dressing room balcony I am slightly wondering why everyone is standing there waving their arms and shouting 'GET BACK. GET BAAACK!' I turn round and suddenly realise that Ramps is also calling out, this time for another run. I sprint as fast as I can back whence I came, scramble back and dive for the line – safe.

Now then. Here's my chance. I'm really going to make them pay now. You don't drop Tuffers on one and get away with it. Except that Curtly has just taken the new ball. I look down at the pitch and it is not a pretty sight. I get hit everywhere – ribs, legs , the lot and decide that discretion should be the better part of valour. The end is not too long in coming and lyrically described in the local paper thus: 'the retreating Tufnell slapped a catch to cover.' All out 170, trail by 182.

Gratifyingly my batting is suitably honoured by the BBC radio Test Match Special team. They decide that my part in saving the follow on is worthy of the award for the champagne moment. A true all-rounder, I have now earned the award for my batting and fielding, as well as my bowling. Quite right, too. Full marks to Ramps (I should be a headline writer). He batted brilliantly, almost certainly his best innings in the 20 Test matches he's played. Bit of a hero of mine, actually.

But it is almost certainly my batting that has had the inspirational effect on my team-mates. That is the only explanation I can offer for what follows.

When West Indies begin their second innings, with their big lead on this pitch, realistically all they need to do is to bat sensibly and they will set us a target we cannot hope to reach on the now-disintegrating surface.

By the close of play they are 127 for nine.

They are obviously determined to blaze away and put the game out of our reach very quickly and I think that worked against them. Stuart Williams edges his fourth ball to Stewie in the slips off Deano. Sherwin Campbell plays a few crisp shots but is then unlucky to be given out caught at short leg by Ramps off Gus and then a real breakthrough when we get Chanderpaul, after his first innings hundred, first ball. He pushes it into the off side and takes off for a sharp but gettable single. Then out of nowhere Nass pounces, picks up and throws down the stumps at the bowler's end in one movement. Brilliant to watch. They are 32 for three.

On some occasions like this when the opposition has a big lead there can be a tendency to take a fatalistic approach – done by the toss, done by the pitch, let's get this over with. There is no hint of that sort of feeling in our cricket in this session. Even while Lara and Hoops are steadying things either side of tea we feel that if we can just keep them within range we might give ourselves an outside chance. Then a spot of personal satisfaction that has been a long time coming. Lara c Butcher b Tufnell. B.C. boiled in the bag for the first time in the series and the first time in Test cricket. Yes.

Not a wicket I shall forget in a hurry. He comes down the

wicket to drive me, realises he isn't quite at the pitch of the ball (done in the flight, of course), then decides to block the ball, which goes off bat to pad and to Butch at silly point. Then, after the drought, the deluge. Hoops becomes the first of three West Indies batsmen to be given out leg before padding up, he to Deano and two later on, Amby and Adams, both to Crofty. In the middle is the best wicket of the lot, in my humble opinion.

Ramps, on for me, sends down his second ball. It is either a rank long-hop or cunningly disguised non-turning length-extender, depending on your perspective. David Williams cracks it towards square leg where the fielder, squinting into the sun, lives up to his nickname by pulling off a miraculous diving catch. I thank you. Call me Bonetti.

The picky ones in the dressing room considered I should have worked on my follow-through camera close-up. A full frame picture of my backside would appeal to only a very few, I fear.

Excellent performance, showing a lot of fight and scrap. We hung in and threw ourselves around, took some good catches and deserved the bit of luck that came our way. They are still 309 ahead BUT if we can only nip one of Ian Bishop and Ramnarine out early tomorrow and bat like angels, we can still win this game.

Monday 2 March. Fourth Test. Day 4

Close of play: est indies 2nd inns 197 all out; England 2nd inns 137 all out. (Tufnell 0*)
Wet Indies won by 242 runs. West ndies 2, England 1.
And then we suffer the classic nightmare of a last-wicket partnership. True, Ramnarine and Bishop chance their arm and played a few shots and good luck to them. Yes, sometimes it is awkward bowling to tailenders who have

nothing to lose. They'll have the odd hack and the ball will travel to strange unexpected places and suddenly they will just start to get away from you.

But did we go out there subconsciously believing that the job had already been done? Did we wait for the wicket to fall rather than make it happen? Bishop hit me for a six over long-on I do not particularly care to recall, and Ramnarine seemed to grow in confidence as time passed. We had a couple of chances put down, but our margin for error was so narrow. If it didn't happen immediately for us the target we required to win was soon going to assume massive proportions. As they racked up seventy sodding runs for the final wicket, that is exactly what happened.

Having dragged the game back we are so disappointed. It just seems that on so many occasions we travel so far, then just fail to take the final step. Up, down, up, down. They should install a new ride at Alton Towers and call it: 'playing Test cricket for England.'

And now, needing a ludicrous 380 to win or the best part of two days to survive for the draw, it's down, down.

Ambrose and Walsh, who else?, do the damage. Ath gets another low score and Amby does him again for the fourth time in seven encounters, this time for one. Outwardly Ath is showing no signs of the pressure but he is in a bad trot and must be suffering. The giant is bowling brilliantly now. Alec later says it is the best spell he has experienced from him and the Windies bowlers just do not allow anyone to really get in. Ramps top scores for the second time in the match and Jack does well to stay in for an hour and forty minutes, but by the time I get out there the match is gone.

The feeling is one of 'just what on earth am I doing out here?' Big West Indies crowd, Curtly and Courtney and a day and a bit to survive with just me and Deano at the wicket.

Quite intimidating. Deano comes out to greet me and says something along the lines of 'let's try and stay out here as long as we can', but I'm not sure I am listening all that hard to be honest. One look at the pitch tells me all I need to know about my prospects for long-term survival. Dean also says: 'I think I'll stay down this end' and as he points to the other end of the track I understood why. There are bits of pitch sitting on top of the main body of it. It is a sort of mosaic of cracks and lumps, almost like a pebble beach. No thanks.

Dean fends off a few and so do I. Then he nicks one, there is a big roar and off we go.

We do feel it was a a win-the-toss-win-the-game situation, but that having been said it is gutting to lose it. Not only because we had dragged ourselves back into contention a couple of times but also because there was a feeling that this was the last thing we deserved having worked so hard to win the last Test in Trinidad. Nothing left for it but to get very very drunk on copious quantities of rum.

There were a few what-ifs and so on, and we try to take out of the match what we can. Try to glean exactly what Athers and Bumble are now thinking. They are down but they try to impress on us that we simply have not had the luck and we do feel this is true.

This was Athers' 50th Test as captain. He claims all these records mean little to him, but we all know how much it means to him for England to do well. Stubborn, cussed etc. yes. But beneath everything, a top bloke. There are suggestions that if we do not win out here, or at least draw, then he will give it away. That's up to him. At least we now know exactly what our task is for the remaining two Tests in Barbados and Antigua. To win the series, we must win both. And, with the support that will now arrive in British Airways Jumbo loads, we really do feel we can.

Tuesday 3 March

Notice the local paper giving the odds now as 20–1 against us winning the series. The West Indies are 10–1 on!

Just Fancy That … skimming through the local paper my eye happens to be caught by the horoscope section, entitled: 'Starscope'. Those with long memories will recall that, back on Friday, January 9, I resolved never again on this trip to even glance at my horoscope entry, as a result of reading the far-from encouraging line: 'You should be most concerned with your professional accomplishments.' Imagine my surprise, then, to read the following entry for today, Tuesday, March 3: 'Taurus: You should be most concerned with your professional accomplishments…' Start to wonder if the same message has been used every day in between.

Looking forward to getting away from the Mozzies, I must admit.

Wednesday 4 March. Guyana to Bridgetown, Barbados

Bad morning at Black Rock. Bad head. Bad. But today we depart Guyana for Barbados. Play with the name a bit as this is the place we love to go. Baah-bay-does, we love it.

Four years ago this was where we stopped being hammered. Three-nil down after three (Jamaica, Guyana and Trinidad – don't mention the 46) we arrived here expected (and expecting?) to be beaten. But over the five days the mood changed totally. Alec batted fantastically well to make hundreds in both innings, the first England Test player to do that against West Indies ever and we went and won in Bridgetown where no visiting Test side had won for 59 years.

Spirits also pepped up by the knowledge that wives,

girlfriends and kids will be there. I've really missed Lisa. Never thought I'd find the sight of Dean Headley in a dress so, shall we say, distracting. As for Poppy, she was a little bundle last time I saw her. Try to imagine what she is going to look like now. Will she recognise me?

Check in to the Club Rockley resort and find out. She takes a few minutes, it has to be said, but the moment I light up a Benson this huge wide smile almost cracks her face in two. She's now got a brush of sticking up white hair, her blue eyes are shining and she looks good enough to eat. Lisa, of course, always does. (The Leslie Phillips approach does it every time, I find)

Lovely, lovely. Then, looking around the place, start to take in the fact that the Brits have arrived in force. Everywhere you go in the complex there are pale pink white people. We love their support, don't get me wrong, but I sometimes wish they'd get a tan before they come out here.

More welcome news is that I am likely to have a break now. Athers is also contemplating missing the match against Barbados. He was always planning to do this, I think, and Izzy is coming over from Guyana so that they can spend some time together somewhere other than in Georgetown. Apparently some of the press have written that he should play in the match in order to try and get back in nick, but I personally think the rest is what he needs.

Controversy raging locally over the fact that the West Indies Board has so far refused to allow the Test match to be broadcast live on the Caribbean Broadcasting Company station. This seems a bit harsh bearing in mind the fact that the Oval has been sold out for months and that a vast number of the allocation was pre-sold to British tourists. No less a personage than the great E.W.Swanton has become involved. The Nation newspaper has printed Swanton's letter urging the Board to think again. You can almost hear the scurrying start.

Thursday 5 March

Day off for all. Gratefully received. Down to the beach at Rockley, with Lisa and Poppy. Apart from the rainy trip to Maracas the day after losing the second Test in Trinidad, this is the first time I or any of the lads have seen a bathing beach since January 18th, when we finished off the match in Montego Bay, Jamaica. That was forty-five days ago, six and a half weeks. No-one is complaining, but the reality of a tour of the Caribbean is not the cocktail of sun, sand, sea and palm trees with the occasional cricket match thrown in some people might still have in their heads Good fun though Kingston, Port-of-Spain and Georgetown undoubtedly are, they would be no-one's choice for a holiday in the sun. Well, not mine anyway.

Interestingly, find out later that Athers and Nasser decided on a spot of extra practice today. Ath has been doing his best not to let his run of scores interfere with the captaincy and is trying to remain upbeat and positive. But it doesn't half help if you are making a big contribution yourself. Up at the Wanderers Club, round the corner from the complex, a few local bowlers from Pickwick CC have been recruited to put Ath and Nass through their paces. This has apparently been kept secret from the media. Typical that Ath would want to go about his business in private without making a song and dance about his extra work.

Bumble is doing his best to keep Ath's spirits up, but both of them have been here before, in Zimbabwe and New Zealand last year. Then Ath turned things round and made millions against the Kiwis. Now ? In the local paper Bumble has been quoted as saying: 'Atherton's form is not a concern.

175

When you come up against Ambrose and Walsh on what are considered bowler-friendly pitches, you have got a severe examination. Nobody would tell whether your players are in form or not.' Four years ago, on his first tour as captain, Ath made 510 Test runs at an average of 56.66. So far this time he has made 96 from seven innings and he hasn't made a Test fifty since the second innings of the second Test against Australia at Lord's, fifteen knocks ago. He knows things can turn around in a blink, but he sets himself high standards and the longer he goes without a score, the more it must hurt him and us.

Friday 6 March

Confirmed that I am being rested for tomorrow's match against Barbados at the Kensington Oval. They didn't ask me if I wanted a rest, and that is the way I prefer it. We all play cricket for enjoyment as well as for a living, but I would be lying if I didn't say that occasionally, just occasionally, the prospect of another game is about as appealing as a cup of cold sick. No-one is ever going to say I don't want to play, so in that situation all you can do is hope that the right messages have got through. This time they have.

Athers tells the press boys that he hasn't made up his mind yet about whether he is going to play, but I suspect this is not entirely accurate.

Pop down to the ground today for a look at the square. Can't really tell, but all the signs indicate that, at last, we will be playing on some proper batting surfaces.

Swanton has spoken, the West Indies Board has heard. The match is going to be on local telly, after all. Once E.W.S. intervened, the outcome, of course, was never in doubt.

Now that I know I am not playing try out a couple of the bars that four years ago I may have popped into once or

176

Curtly Rules, OK. Windies' Man of the Series, King Curt,
sends Jack Russell on his way.

Left: Athers tried to separate his personal batting problems from the job of leading the side. But in the end he decided enough was enough.

Below: Yes, believe it or not, a rare occasion on tour when beachwork took precedence, Rockley Bay, Barbados.

Left: Happy families with Lisa and Poppy during a very welcome weekend off in Barbados.

Above: Co-author Peter Hayter, under *Mail on Sunday* Editor's orders to sample the authentic Caribbean atmosphere and several litres of Mount Gay rum on the first day of the Barbados Test.

Below: The Beach Bar at Rockley Beach, advertising my kind of job.

Above: Derek Pringle pauses to break wind after eating an entire boat.

Below: Music maestro, please. But turn down those drums, man.

The Barmy Army. Loud and proud … … but the Trini Posse move a little better.

Ambrose is too quick for Athers as the England captain faces the chin music during the first innings of the 5th Test in Bridgetown.

Graham Thorpe drives Curtly Ambrose on his way to a century on day two of the fifth Test.

A triumphant moment at the Kensington Oval for Ramps, who cuts Nixon McLean to the boundary to bring up his 150 for England ...

... only for the team to have our hopes dashed by rain on the final day. Is this Manchester or Barbados?

A tactical decision is being hammered out by me and Nasser on the eve of the sixth and final Test in Antigua. In the end, we plump for the lobster.

'Gravy' stirring up a party in Antigua as the West Indies clinch another Test and series victory.

Above: I'm last man out, even if I don't realise it, as the West Indies celebrate winning the final Test.

Below: Suggestion: why don't we pack these two off on a boat round the world, so that next time England come to the Caribbean they WILL have retired.

twice ... Harbour Lights, The Boatyard, The Ship, legendary names among the barmies and other travelling England supporters. They are absolutely heaving already and the main invasion force hasn't even arrived yet. Next week is going to be pandemonium.

Saturday 7 March

Great pitch. They get a shedload. One ball does something out of the ordinary, a delivery from Chris Silverwood which flies off a length and all but decapitates Sherwin Campbell. Taking evasive action he gloves it to Jack. Poor bloke. He is a good player in a bat trot and this won't help. Clayton Lambert and Philo Wallace, Campbell's Bajan opening partner are being pushed in some quarters to replace him and Stuart Williams. Wallace smacks a very forceful 68 here, hitting the ball extremely hard, and the other fellah bound to play by all accounts, Roland Holder, scores a hundred. Following his 183 against us for West Indies A at Chedwin Park back in January, he has netted another 115 not out as they made 328 for four in the day. If he makes the XI this might be a good time to try out plan B.

Out to dinner with Lisa, my sensible brother Greg and his wife Emma who are over for a visit and the cricket. We go to the wonderful Carambola restaurant on the West coast just north of Bridgetown. Brilliant place, built into a cliff with a network of wooden stairs connecting the different levels. The sound of the waves crashing 50 feet below and the candlelight etc, have been known to do the trick. Gazing into Liza's eyes it's just possible I might be in with a shout. The evening starts badly when I drop my fags over the edge of the balcony and ponder whether to climb down the cliff to retrieve them, and progresses in spectacular fashion when a large flying insect dive-bombs Lisa and ends up getting entangled in the barnet. She freaks completely, pulling at her hair wildly and waving her arms about while we all sit there like lemons, with our menu on top of our heads. The situation does not improve when someone on another table screams "IT'S A BAT! IT'S A BAT!!" at which Lisa nearly faints. Waiters are summoned, plates sent flying and by this time everyone in the entire restaurant is absorbed in this titanic struggle between my wife and the THING. Finally this huge moth flaps its gigantic wings and flutters away into the night quite oblivious to the carnage it has left behind. Lisa calms down quickly but insists that, from now on you can stick your al fresco dining thank you very much, she will be inside.

Thereafter any further attempts at amore this evening prove utterly futile.

Sunday 8 March

And on they bat today. Holder makes 158 before being run out. That's 341 runs in two innings, average 170.5. They make 472 for six declared. And the batting practice continues when we go in.

Monday 9 March

And there's more. We make 382.

West Indies announce their squad. They've seen the pitch. Lambert – big licks, man, is in. So is Wallace – even bigger licks. Holder is in as well. Lambert will be the oldest man on the pitch at 36, playing his second Test six years after his first … at the Oval in 1991 I seem to recall. Wallace and Gromit (sorry, Lambert) will be their tenth opening partnership in seven years, which just goes to emphasise how outstanding was the great Gordon Greenidge – Desmond Haynes pairing, for many people the best ever.

A few whispers in the press that I might be dropped for the Test match in favour of Crofty. Also some discussion about Alec keeping and both of us playing. Can't think Alec will keep because that would mean him dropping down the order from opening where four years ago on this ground he scored centuries in both innings to help win the Test match and become a god of cricket. I find it disappointing but not surprising. I feel on balance I have bowled well this series. It just irritates the shit out of me and all of us that we are arriving here 2–1 down when we could and we feel we should be 2–1 up.

Now we will have to make sure we get our reward.

Tuesday 10 March

More practice and big fun in the evening where we are invited to see how the other half live – and this time I do not mean Bob Bennett.

We have been invited to a party at the Barbados residence of Robert Sangster in aid of local orphans. Unofficial King of British racing, some say. Bagsawonga, say others. His house is amazing, all columns and porticoes and the like. Not many walls, as a matter of fact. And views of the sea you would like to put on your bedroom wall and die to. People have paid US$100 for the privilege of a drink and a chat with us with the proceeds to the charity. Sangster is a good bloke and a bit of a liver, by all accounts. Beefy knows him well. Say no more. The highlight of the evening is the show put on by England's greatest all-rounder and Sangster's black Labrador, Archie. Steady.

The trick is this: Beefy picks up a golf ball and throws it into the swimming pool which is all lit up. Archie runs along the diving board and jumps in. He swims around until he can see the ball on the floor of the pool, then dives right down, somehow WALKS along the bottom, then collects the ball and swims back to the surface. We suggest that Archie and Beefy should reverse roles. The beast is unenthusiastic. And Archie is not too keen either.

Rather too much champagne, perhaps ... but it was all drunk for charity.

CHAPTER NINE

*A shower of s**t*

Wednesday 11 March

The build-up is really starting to get hold of us now. You can feel the excitement and tension growing within the large number of supporters who are staying at our place. They come for the sun and the sea and the rum as well, of course, but the cricket is the real reason why we are all here.

There are downsides, naturally. Not being overly snotty about this but having to join a mile-long queue for food tonight is not perhaps the kind of experience that international sportsmen in other disciplines find themselves involved in. And the second aspect is the chat. These people are very genuine and they put their hands in their pockets time after time for the privilege, but the kind of things they say to you most often are: 'You've really got to win tomorrow,' or 'We really want you to try this time,' and what can you say in reply?

Being peered at by total strangers can be a little disconcerting at times too. After a while you get used to it, but my sympathies to all those in the monkey-house at London Zoo.

The team meeting starts with a bang. Bob Bennett rises to his feet and thanks us for participating in the Sangster event and announces that around US$100,000 has been raised for the orphan kids. 'These children live only a mile or two away from the beach and yet some have never even seen the sea,' he says.

'What have we done then, bought them a map?', enquires one of the more uncouth members of the squad. Very fifth form.

The team is announced. Crofty is omitted in favour of Andy Caddick. I thought Robbo bowled well in Guyana and, knowing how these things work there must have been some discussion over whether, if we were going to go in with only one spinner, it should have been him. The fact that both the new local paper, the *Barbados Advocate*, as well as most of the papers back in England I later discover, has written that I am the one for the chop, means that some little bird has been flying around whispering in a few ears. Had Alec kept we could both have played AND Caddick. Nothing I can do about it, though.

The rest of the meeting proceeds along the usual lines, but this time there are fresh things to discuss, like the new players. We talk through Lambert and Wallace, the fact that they can come out swinging from the hip and that if carnage does ensue we must be ready just to stay with it. Not to worry about Guyana is probably the strongest message that Ath and Bumble are giving us.

Everyone is aware of the importance of the cricket we are to play between now and the end of the series. At the climax of a mission that began on 3 January, sixty-eight days ago, the success of all of our efforts is going to judged on what happens in the next fortnight. We are 2–1 down and we feel we do not deserve to be, but all the moral victories and sessions where we have played the better cricket will count for nothing unless we manage to achieve some kind of positive result here in Barbados and Antigua. If we win both, we will return home in triumph as the players who won for England here for the first time in most of our lifetimes. If we get a 2–2 draw out of the series, that will do nicely as well. But if it were to go pear shaped now, no-one will remember the dropped catches, the decisions that went against us or the bad luck we have had with the toss on crucial occasions. We will simply be branded as losers.

Everyone is feeling for Ath. He has looked okay in the nets this week and no-one could have worked harder. But a bad trot for a Test captain means more than a bad trot for any other Test batsman. And after having allowed himself to be persuaded to carry on in the job at the end of last summer, when the press subjected him to the usual badgering, he can expect more of the same if we do not win here. Whether accurate or not, the assessment of most pundits at the start of this tour was that a) West Indies, having been thrashed by Pakistan and seemingly torn apart by internal squabbling, were there for the taking, and b) England, having ended the Ashes series on a high note, were more than capable of taking them. What is more, Athers must have felt that way too, or he would not have put himself through the whole business again. We all respect him hugely and he is a mate as well as our skipper. And some of us – namely Gus, Jack, Ramps and Nass – owe our return to Test cricket to his judgement against the views of a former chairman of selectors who could be mentioned, so there is a lot of emotion involved here. There is a feeling within the team that we want to do well now not just for ourselves and England, but also for Ath.

Thursday 12 March, Fifth Test, Kensington Oval, Day 1
Close of play: England 1st inns 229–5 (Ramprakash 80*, Thorpe 50*)
So, farewell then, Lloyd Bridges.

Looks like I picked the wrong day to give up sniffing glue.
That was your catchphrase.
We are all sniffing now.

Sad news. Lloyd Bridges, star of *Airplane* has died aged 85.

Travelling to the ground this morning through the crowds of punters carrying their Union Jacks and other flags, was a bit like how it must be for the England footballers driving down Wembley Way. I remember a similar scene from four years ago but this was something else. Nerves jangling now, and heart beating a beat faster, but the energy is positive rather than draining. This is the kind of thing you play cricket for.

On arrival certain players who shall remain nameless (Alec Stewart, Angus Fraser, Mike Atherton) make straight for the areas of the dressing-room they used on our last Test match visit here. Being a bit slower off the mark, I feign total disregard for this pathetic superstition but finally find somewhere to park myself.

The boys are so up for this now that the feeling almost irritates the skin. The batsmen have seen the pitch and they like what they see. At last, after the Russian Roulette at Sabina Park, the sideways movement and up-and-downness of Queen's Park Oval and the crumbling dust bowl at the Bourda, they must be thinking, thank God for something we can actually look to bat on normally. And they get their chance when Lara wins the toss and inserts us again. Interesting. There are some captains who, sitting on a 2–1 lead with two Tests to play, might consider the best way of closing down the possibility of losing the series would be to bat the opposition out of the game. If they were to bat first and make 400 on what looks like a belter, how can we win from there? This way, if we make a big first innings score, we give ourselves the chance of victory. Lara's tactic suggests he has no such thoughts in his head. So far in the series his key weapons have been Ambrose and Walsh and he is backing them to do the job again. I suppose what would also be in his head is that if this pitch is going to do anything at all it will probably do it in the first session.

Game on. Well, almost. Somewhat of an anti-climax for the packed house and for the players when Courtney, standing at the end of his run and preparing to send down the first delivery in the middle of huge noise, notices something awry with the ball. He shows it to Lara and they both ask the umpires Cyril Mitchley and Eddie Nicholls for it to be changed. Ten minutes later, we finally get underway.

By lunchtime all our hopes of a victory to rank alongside 1994 seem to have been snuffed out like a fag in a bottle of beer. We are 55 for four – Athers, Alec, Butch and Nass are all out. Chalks is lying on the physio's couch with a buggered back and, assuming he can actually bat again, we have only him and Ramps left of the senior specialist batters.

Perhaps the boys are slightly over-confident or guilty of trying to take charge too soon, but all of them look in good nick until they get out. Al first, driving at Courtney and caught behind at 23 for one. Sometimes he is in such commanding form that he gets himself in two minds whether to keep playing shots or tone down the power. Make that 24 for two. Ath's terrible run continues. He takes on Courtney's bouncer, hooks, top-edges and then suffers that agonising second-and-a-half gazing up in the sky and down at the fielder before Amby devours it 20 yards in from the long leg boundary.

Lara continues to surprise. He takes Amby out of their attack after four overs. Why? Don't ask me. Is the breeze too strong for the great man? Whatever, it works. Nixon

McLean (is he Thunder or Lightning? I never can get it right), runs in bowling real fast, sends two short snorters towards Nass's snotbox and gets him with the second, caught by Lara at 33 for three. Slight uneasy feelings creeping into the dressing room banter, now. We are not going to get rolled here, now, for God's sake.

Now what? Chalks is feeling his back. The fizz jigs out to treat him and return looking concerned. Chalks carries on and with Butch starts to repair the damage to the innings. They cut down on the shots and just accumulate for a period. But he is clearly struggling. Then Amby comes back on and gets Butch caught in the slips and the next thing we see is Chalks summoning Morton back onto the field then collapsing to the ground. That'd be handy. Four down for nothing and Chalks out of the game.

Ramps walks out into crisis for the third time in three innings. Chalks stays on for the time being, then Ramps has one of those moments on which a career can turn. On five, in the over before lunch, he is squared up by Amby and sends back a return catch low to his left. Amby stoops, gets a paw to it but just can't quite hold on. Just imagine if he caught the ball. England 60-odd for five, Chalks struggling. Ramps maybe branded a choker again – with what consequences inside his head? – and the rest history.

But this time the people who makes these decisions say: 'Go on. We'll give you this one. See what you make of it.'

Nothing much yet. Chalks is the centre of attention in the break. He has a problem moving his legs. When he puts any weight on his front leg, the back goes into a sort of spasm and the pain stops him from putting his foot down. Lots of treatment and finally an injection during the interval. He will not be going anywhere for a while, so Jack is sent in to replace him and proceeds to play a small innings of immense

186

importance. For one thing, our supporters really respond to seeing Jack, as they always do. They love him for being a little battler. He's a complete raving lunatic, of course, what with his obsessions over diet and all things military – in fact had he been born any other era I am convinced he would have been cannon fodder – but he is, with every atom in his body, the bloke for the backs-to-the-wall scenario. Inscrutable behind his shades and carrying a bat that looks at least three sizes too big for him to carry, he gives the impression that he would happily lay down his life rather than be got out. Eight years ago he did everything but the last full stop of the job to bat England to the draw here that would have given them at least a share of the series, but with the target in sight, Curtly Ambrose did him with a grubber with his first delivery using the new ball. The second best defensive innings I have ever seen, although I only watched it on the box, was his effort alongside Athers' 185 not out in the second Test against South Africa at the Wanderers in 1995. The English punters are not the only ones who believe that if anyone can get us out of this mess, Jack is yer man.

Bugger me if he doesn't just go out and dominate the match. He takes Courtney on, in true scuttling style, with loads of staring and growling thrown in which winds up his Gloucestershire team-mate and gets everyone going even more, and suddenly the state of the game is forgotten. Brilliant stuff.

His belligerence allows Ramps just to settle and take things at his own pace. Maybe whatever dampness had been in the pitch early on had now also disappeared. But from 53 for four, Jack's scrapping 32 has just taken us out of the embarrassment zone. What is more Jack has bought Chalks some time. Had Jack come and gone cheaply and the tail followed suit, Chalks might not have had the chance to come back out. This way he has an hour and a half of further treatment so that when Jack is finally out at 153 for five, he sits up and says: 'Yeah. I'm going back in.' And then he and Ramps just go and bat superbly.

Maybe the runs he made in the previous match help Ramps here. But nothing has flustered him, not going in facing a firing squad, not getting away with a dropped catch early on, not Chalks being unable to carry on after lunch, nothing. I've seen him play like this a million times for Middlesex and it has always baffled me why he has not been given a longer run to try and establish himself at Test level. I know how cut up he was to be out of the frame at the start of the tour and now you can see the determination in everything he does. At the close we are 229 for five, with Ramps eighty not out and Chalks just reaching his fifty. Magnificent effort. In a match we must win but which could so easily have been out of reach, we are still competing. And how must they be feeling?

At the end of the day's play I notice something utterly remarkable. The 56 minutes at Sabina Park apart, this is the first day of the Test series when I haven't been on the field of play at all.

Friday 13 March, Fifth Test, Day 2

England 1st inns 403 all out; West Indies 1st inns 84–1 (Lambert 32*, Bishop 2*)

Bumped into the Judge, last night. No, no. Don't panic. Not that sort of judge. Robin Smith (new readers start here – 'Judge' is his nickname), my mucker from recent tours past who, currently not in favour with the selectors, is out here leading a party of punters. Some merriment has recently been caused by an open letter written by his wife Kath to the chairman of selectors David Graveney that appeared in full in the *Mail On Sunday* last weekend. It was all Dear Mr. Graveney, why are you being so beastly to my husband? Mainly tongue in cheek, I suspect, but also quite pointed. What has caused the most mirth among the boys and encouraged some mild urine extraction is the story she recounted concerning the pair of them at a recent cricket luncheon. Apparently, Kath was slightly bored so she decided to flick a scoop of ice cream at her husband, as you do. Robin saw it early and dodged out of the way as it flew harmlessly past his nose and landed on an adjoining table. And this simple test proved, according to Kath, that his reflexes for dealing with everything the Windies pacemen had to offer were as sharp as ever. Wonder what flavour Curtly and Courtney will be bowling today?

We all love the Judge and I've watched him take the blows against these blokes and come back for more. Hope that we haven't seen the last of him.

But for now all eyes are on Ramps and Chalks. We are in a far better state than we were at 53 for four, i.e. still alive, however … if we were to lose an early wicket this morning we could still find ourselves in shtuck. But when Ramps hits Courtney through cover for four early on you can hear the collective breathing-out in the dressing room. Chalks, now pretty much fully recovered, collects unfussily as well. And then comes one of the most misty-eyed moments of my career, Ramps reaching his first Test hundred. Great shot, too, leaning back and cracking young Nixon through extra cover off the back foot to the boundary.

What goes through a bloke's mind in a situation like this?

You have confidence in your own talent, of course you do. But until you get the score on the door, the gap between capability and performance is never closed. Now Ramps knows he can do it because he *has* done it. I'm looking hard at his face for any sign of what's going on behind it and the smile as wide as the Grand Canyon that seems stuck there just says relief. I wasn't wrong to believe in myself after all, and neither were you who supported me.

There have been a few doubters. Even, from time to time, himself. Not any more.

Chalks's hundred is no less worthy an effort, bearing in mind the pain he was suffering early on. Chalks is my little-legged mate. Unflappable, calm, soothing influence. The bloke I go to, to chill out with. He has a way of putting things in the correct order, the proper perspective. Fiercely committed to his game and dedicated, but able to mentally switch off from the game when necessary. Very funny bloke, too, in his moments, but his lack of real success on this trip must have been getting to him slightly. His reward for batting on a few dodgy ones is this pitch. No wonder he was so desperate to get back on the field.

The partnership ends when Chalks is out soon after making three figures, but this has been sensational cricket for us. For the first time in the series the atmosphere in our dressing room while we have been batting has been something other than anxiety verging on panic. Instead of living on my nerves, watching every ball on the telly, thinking oh Christ that kept low, oh Christ I'm in, this time I've had a chance of some zs, got some scoff down the neck, sat with my feet up and generally swanned about a bit ... all vital elements in the life of a bowler, I can assure you, and especially yours truly.

This stand of 205 is a record sixth wicket partnership for England against West Indies. And for most of its duration the only dressing room tension has been the fight between me and Fraze over whose turn it is to kip on the physio's couch. The feelgood factor has even encouraged the boys to relax enough to indulge in a couple of top-class dressing-room pranks, formulated and carried off with great aplomb by Big Ash and his co-non-playing-through-no-fault-of-his-own tourist Chris Silverwood. It has been very hard for them to go through this trip with so little cricket and even harder that, while not playing, they have been subjected to rigorous fitness work by the maniac Dean Riddle. A large part of all this has been intensive work with the dumbells (weights, I think they call them these days), so the lads devise a plan to gain revenge. They call Riddle into the shower room for another session and he bends down to lift the dumbells, totally unaware that these scallywags have superglued them to the floor.

The second victims of Silverwood and Ashley's rascalry are me and Creeps. The clean livers have insisted that, during intervals, we smokers should be banned from lighting up in the dressing room. Instead, we have been banished to the showers. Unbeknown to us, Ash and Silvers have been busy rigging up some Heath Robinson-style contraption designed to underline the error of our ways. They have sellotaped a length of fishing wire to each of the shower handles and lie in wait. So there are me and Creeps sitting in the cubicles, puffing away happily and nattering about the meaning of life when suddenly, one tug of the fishing line and we are both absolutely soaked to the skin.

Kids, do not try this at home.

On the field, things are now progressing smoothly. By the time Ramps finally goes he has set another record. His 154 is the highest ever by an Englishman here. After all that has happened in his career, nine hours at the crease at the Kensington Oval have made him, for the moment, a piece of history.

Thereafter Deano makes a handy 32 to help us reach our

final total of 403, a score which would have been quite unimaginable before lunch yesterday, the tailenders having left the scene without too much more ado. Now it is up to us to try and fulfil our part of the bargain with the ball.

Against the new opening pair of Lambert and Wallace we do quietly fancy that we can make inroads.

Ahem. No-one expected them to come with silencers on their bats, but this is gunslinging of the highest order as they smash it to all parts. Wallace was particularly pumped up. Some of his shots are top-class, others are close to heaves, but his game plan is to try and belt them back into the game and when you play positively it's amazing how often the luck goes with you. I think one or two of the boys might have pointed this out to Philo, in a gentle way, of course, and that might have been the thing that started the events that seemed to me to fill up a disproportionate amount of space in the newspapers back home over the following few days.

Certainly, the atmosphere inside the ground was super-charged. The West Indies supporters, disappointed that we had got ourselves off the hook and no doubt rather irritated by watching our batters get the upper hand, were absolutely loving every second of this batting assault, particularly as the man at the centre of it, Philo Wallace was a Bajan and one of their own.

From my fielding position on the long leg boundary in front of the Trini Posse, the noise was deafening. In between overs they cranked up the sound system and let rip with the scary bull charge: 'Toro.'

'If yuh have the mad bull fever, yuh have the mad bull fever
If yuh have the mad bull fever, yuh have the mad bull fever
If yuh have the mad bull fever, yuh have the mad bull fever

Yuh have it, yuh have it

EVERYBODY CHARGE!
'TORO TORO – CHARGE
TORO TORO – CHARGE
TORO TORO – CHARGE
TORO TORO – CHARGE.'

The lyrics may leave something to be desired but, to be honest, I don't think anyone was listening to the words. The song is hot and heavy enough without them. Inevitably players get into the atmosphere and it can carry you away.

This is the story: Deano and Philo had been having a little dig at each other. Philo got the upper hand at one stage by striking him for three fours in one over and when Dean won a touch-and-go leg before shout against his opponent, given out by Cyril Mitchley, he wasn't all that keen to depart the playing area.

At this point Athers, running up to congratulate his bowler and celebrate the breakthrough, gave physical expression to the feeling almost all of us had in our hearts and minds. Something along the lines of: 'Whatever you may think, mate, the umpire has given you out. Now, on your bike.' It happened in the blink of an eye, too fast and at the wrong angle for television cameras to pick it up, but, unfortunately, not fast enough to escape the lens of one solitary press photographer, the veteran Kiwi snapper, Ross Setford, covering the tour for the Empics agency.

For the time being we were, simply, delighted to see the back of Wallace after his 45 from only 48 balls and his opening stand of 82 with Lambert that had slightly changed the momentum of the game.

Nothing more was thought or said about the incident that

evening, for the simple reason that we had no idea that it was going to become an incident at all.

Saturday 14 March, Fifth Test, Day 3

West Indies 1st inns 262 all out; England 2nd inns 2–0 (Atherton 2*, Stewart 0*)

The media is already in full kerfuffle when we arrive at the ground. Back home a photograph has appeared in the late edition of *The Sun* showing Athers apparently flicking a V-sign at Wallace. It is not pretty, but I have seen far worse. Nothing meant by these gestures, and if there is any animosity between players on the field in the heat of the moment, these things are usually sorted out afterwards in private over a beer. But Bob Bennett is sufficiently concerned about the reaction of the press guys today, once the photo starts appearing in front of their sports editors back home, to try and head them off at the pass. Through Brian Murgatroyd he issues a statement indicating that he is satisfied that no malice or abuse was intended. 'The umpires made no complaint and the home side made no complaint and as far as we are concerned the matter is closed,' said Murgers.

Well, sadly, it isn't. A group of the Sunday paper reporters come across the ground before the start of play to interview the match referee Barry Jarman. He tells them that he is not concerned, that he didn't see the V-sign, that the photograph could be showing Athers asking for a guard of 'two legs' from the umpire and generally trying to play the whole thing down. Lord MacLaurin is present and grilled by a couple of the reporters but he also employs the 'didn't see the incident line'. By all accounts, they are not terribly impressed and there is also a rumour doing the rounds that it has been put to some of the Sky team by certain influential Board figures

194

that they might employ their blind eye in considering how much to make of the matter. Hotly denied by all at Sky, I might add. In any case the Sunday reporters think they have more than enough material on which to base a cover-up story and no two words get journalists going like those two. They have an early edition deadline for their reports and if nothing much happens in the morning session this will go a long way to filling the 1,000-word long holes.

Athers is genuinely unfussed, although he does tell some of the guys later that he regretted the gesture as soon as he had done it. He realises that as England captain there are certain things expected (certain people have made the point that it was not the gesture itself but what it might have led to that was potentially problematic, e.g. a counter-reaction from the batsman). And I suppose that if he had made an apology to Philo, the Windies Board or whoever there and then, no-one would have had anything more to moan about. But always for Ath the bottom line has been that our job is to try and win Test matches and if that means hanging tough, as they say in the States, then so be it. This is a passionate game, thank goodness, and yesterday evening passions were very high. Ath also believes firmly that what happens on the pitch should stay on the pitch. And of course that is exactly what would have happened had the sign not been captured so graphically on camera.

Once we are on the field, the only thing we are interested in is bowling them out, which we do, really well, on one of our best days of the entire tour.

First up, Athers' tactics are brilliant. The previous evening I had been able to put the brakes on their scoring, so he decides to start off this morning with me and Ramps bowling his occasional off-spin, which absolutely does Lambert in the brain. In the entire morning session the man who would rather pull out his own teeth with a pair of rusty pliers than play a forward-defensive block scores twelve runs. I bowl tight and tidy but he does not play a shot. Once I get the nightwatchman, Ian Bishop, Lara responds to the situation by taking on Gus and Deano and succeeds up to a point, making 31 out of the 58 they make in the two hours until lunch. Then, clearly frustrated by the fact that we are keeping the screws on, he has a hack at Dean and is snared by Butch at cover.

At the break, I'm looking at figures of one for 15 from 17 overs. Very nice too, but we are all a bit baffled by their approach and after lunch comes more of the same. Chanderpaul decides to play me and Ramps from the crease and labours, Holder comes out, slogs and gets bowled by Ramps for ten and Hoops, coming in at number seven, scratches around for near on an hour and a half for nine. Once he is out, the rest scrabble about until Curtly has a late swing and drags them up to 262 all out.

Now, if you'll allow me a moment of personal satisfaction, here, please, Curtly's demise takes me to the landmark of 100 Test wickets. Bit of a relief, actually. Ever since I got Bishop for the 99th I had been clutching and the harder I tried the more anxious I became. But Jack stumps Curtly by a gnat's whisker and the television replays confirm the lovely moment. I get the impression that some people think I don't take this business all that seriously as to think of records and so forth. They are wrong.

At the close we are 143 on with all ten wickets standing. Top drawer.

Looking back on the day, I think our display was about as good as it could have been. We kept up the pressure all the way through and left them unsure whether to bat positively or try to consolidate – in cricket parlance, they didn't quite know whether to sh** or shave. We did get away with one, to be fair, namely the wicket of Chanderpaul which might have proved crucial. To the naked eye, he drove at a full toss from Fraser and the ball ended up in Alec's hands at slip. From where I was standing, admittedly some distance away, there was something not quite right about the dismissal, but I couldn't really put my finger on what that something was. At any rate, Chanderpaul didn't make any fuss and off he went. But television replays did prove that he was unlucky as they clearly showed that he hit the ball hard into the ground and therefore Alec had merely pulled off a fine piece of fielding rather than a catch. I am pretty certain there is no way that Gus would have known and all Al would have been concerned with was taking the catch cleanly.

All part of the fun. As was my afternoon fielding on the deep square leg boundary in front of the Trini Posse.

It began quite harmlessly with the odd bit of banter and the occasional piece of fruit or chicken whistling past my earhole. In fact, when someone chucked a fag that landed at my feet, I was quite touched. Problem was that once one came my way and a few more of the Posse cottoned onto the idea, it was not long before I was standing under a cloud-burst of Benson & Hedges. Still good larks, etc at this stage and I duly picked them all up and made a neat pile on the other side of the boundary rope. Then – well done, Philip – I went and asked for a light. Next thing I knew I was being pelted with cigarette lighters.

And then came the ice. Not so bad when it started with individual cubes. But when I got hit in the back of the head by a clump of them stuck together things were beginning to get out of hand. Hardly a deadly weapon I grant you, not like the six inch metal bolt that narrowly missed Devon Malcolm in a one-day international at Jamshedpur on our 1993 tour of India, or the full size cricket bat Derek Pringle insists somebody threw at him at Adelaide once. But still enough to give you a bit of a fright.

It was at this stage that I called Athers over and suggested he might have a word with the umpires. I'm all for a the crowd having a bit of a laugh, but there are limits. In answer to your next question, yes, I did keep the fags.

Sunday 15 March, Fifth test, Day 4

England 2nd inns 223–3 dec. (Hussain 46*, Thorpe 36*); West Indies 2nd inns 71–0 (Lambert 28*, Wallace 38*)

By now the Sunday papers have appeared back home. Unfortunately, but predictably, the main story in some of them is still the V-sign, rather than the fact that we have bowled West Indies out and taken command of the Test match. Ath appears well miffed by this, but maybe it increases his desire to finish the job. Whatever, he proceeds to produce his best innings of the series, by a long chalk. He gets 64 in an opening stand of 101 with Al, sticking another two fingers, this time metaphorically, at those who criticised him for missing the game against Barbados, and our boys make runs all the way down the order. After tea Nass and Chalks crack 60 in ten overs which warms the cockles – the sight of the little-legged left-hander hooking King Curt for three successive boundaries into the Kensington Stand was worth coming on tour for.

After which we declare, leaving them 109 overs to make 375 (strangely, the same number of runs with which Lara set the Test record four years ago. Coincidence?) Then, deja vu. Wallace and Lambert do to us this evening exactly what they did to us on Friday. All parts. Carnage. I come on and try to put the net over them again and to an extent it works, but by the close they have cut the target to 304 off 90 overs.

Overnight we are extremely upbeat. Knowing what we know now about how the openers go about things, they are sure to have a crash in the morning and that will put the pressure on Lara to continue going for the runs all day. So if we can make early inroads and they keep coming at us, it could easily be our day.

In fact, at last, it could easily be MY day. Spend the evening thinking about all the hard work I have put in during the tour and how tomorrow may make it all worthwhile. Team game, of course, but once in a while you want the figures, you want the wickets, for yourself. Just fancy a cheeky little five-for here if the rough comes into the equation as we think it will, the match and the 2–2 and one to play.

Monday 16 March, Fifth Test, Day 5

West Indies 2nd inns 112–2 (Lara 13*, Chanderpaul 3*).
Match drawn. West Indies 2, England 1

Thank you, God. Thank you so very much.

Woke up this morning, pulled back the curtains and it can't be, but it is. ABSOLUTELY HOSING DOWN.

This early, there is still plenty of time. But on the way to the ground no-one likes the look of what's coming down. By now we are all used to the short, sharp tropical bursts that come down like Noah's Flood and then disappear in minutes. But this has been coming down for some time and the sky looks strangely sort of , Mancunian. Filled in. Slate grey. No gaps.

At the ground I am welcomed by a local soothsayer who tells me, gleefully, 'No play today'. Thanks very much.

It is very quiet on our dressing room and not very quiet in theirs. In fact the chuckling does not help at all. We try and keep positive, but the over-riding feeling is total despair. This was our chance. On a personal level, this was MY chance. We have come back from a terrible position, outplayed them for four days and are in with a big chance of levelling the series and now this.

David Graveney has been here all match and will stay on next week to run the one-day squad while we are in Antigua. He tries his best to keep spirits up, as does Bumble, and we do get on for brief period. But soon the rain comes again and at twenty past two-ish it is all over. Looking around the dressing room everyone is gutted, everyone.

The effect, as they say, is f***ing shattering. We now cannot win the series, so the target we worked our b******s off for is out of reach. How will this affect us in Antigua? How will this affect Athers? He's put so much into this tour and now, what with the incident on Friday, the vultures are already circling overhead.

Ath has tried to separate his own batting and captaincy worries from the business of motivating us. To be fair, he very rarely deviates from being himself – a bit dour in front of the media boys perhaps, but, and I'm not just saying this, a real quality bloke with his players and friends. No huge mood swings, no violent ups and downs, just Ath.

People who don't know him have accused him of being downbeat and surly. Captain Grumpy, some of them have called him. But that is crap. In company he is a good laugh. In fact from a personal point of view, he has often come in handy on evenings out. A bit like Derek Pringle when I first started, if ever anyone came along with some long-worded insult, Ath would act as interpreter. 'Ath, mate. That bloke just called me a supercilious bastard. What's he on about?'

'Well, Cat,' he would reply quick as a flash, 'Supercilious: displaying arrogant pride, scorn or indifference. From the Latin *superciliosus*, from *supercillium*, meaning eyebrow.'

And away you'd go.

Seriously, there are a lot of people here who are desperate to do well for Ath as well as for themselves. We are all feeling for him now. The knowledge that we are not going to win this series is flooding over people and we are all dying a little.

For the first time on the tour I cannot make out the expression on his face. In Trinidad when we lost the Test we should have won, he was annoyed. In Georgetown when things went against us he looked more resigned than anything else. This time he looks empty. I see Graveney looking at him in silence. All kinds of things are racing around your brain.

As for myself, I do feel a bit cheated. It should have been a nice hot sunny day, a nice pitch to bowl on, offering a bit for me and then more as the rough got rougher and a real total to bowl from. Everyone continues to tell me that I have bowled all right, but do they really mean it? I wanted some wickets so that I could stop wondering. I wanted to win this Test match.

This sodding game.

My day is complete when, at the team meeting in the evening to announce the squad for the one-day international matches at the end of the Test series, my name is absent from the list. No real surprise there as I seem to have been permanently ruled out of contention for the one-day side. It's up to the selectors of course, but I do find the decision a tad ironic bearing in my mind that the last time I played for England in this type of cricket – the first one-day international against New Zealand in Christchurch last February – I finished with figures of four from 22 from ten overs (of five wickets taken) and the Man of the Match award.

CHAPTER TEN

Bye, Bye

Tuesday 17 March. Barbados to Jolly Harbour, Antigua

Don't ask. Up early for flight to Antigua. Lisa's gone home with Poppy. I'm not happy.

Wednesday 18 March

Get up early and slowly come around. So much has happened since we were last here at the Jolly Harbour apartments. The early-tour euphoria seems a long way away now. Not that we have given up, not by a long chalk. It is just that we are somewhat knackered. For the first time tourists, any visions they might have had of endless days in paradise have been well and truly dispelled and for the vets, there is an ominous feeling that we have been down this road before.

Yes, we can make it 2–2. BUT, they can make it 3–1 and if that happens, not only would it not be a fair reflection as far as we are concerned, it will also be a right, royal pain in the arse. And what will Athers do, then?

Stroll to the end of the beach for lunch with co-author at Coco's restaurant perched on the cliff and overlooking the bay. Incidentally, the other main difference between now and that day in 1973 when we arrived in Antigua is the weather. Last time we ate here the rain was beating so hard that the roof looked like it would buckle. Now the sun is hot and the sky cloudless. The view from our table, across Jolly Bay and out to sea, is priceless.

Nod hello to Ath and Fraze who are dining nearby. They are good mates, always have been since they both made their Test debut in the same season, 1989 versus the Australians. Much later I discover what they are talking about. Whatever happens in the Test match, Ath is unsure whether he should captain the one-day side, feeling that it might be unfair to step into Adam's shoes after what he achieved leading the boys to victory in the Champions Cup in Sharjah. Nothing about the main job, though, yet.

In the evening we happily accept an invitation to join Sir Paul Getty on his yacht which is moored in St John's harbour. One week Sangster, the next week Getty. With my reputation? As well as being inordinately rich, Mr. Getty is one of cricket's largely silent benefactors. In his back garden at home in Worsley, deep in the Oxfordshire countryside he has built a full size cricket pitch, with a gorgeous pavilion, scorebox etc. and simply adores the game. His boat is something else. Right out of the 1920s, it looks like the set for an Hercule Poirot mystery. In fact you can just imagine Peter Ustinov gathering everyone together in the dining room, switching the lights on and off and announcing: 'It eez you, Frau von Roken, n'est-ce pas?'...

The captain gives us a little tour, below decks and above. More jacuzzis than you can count and everything gleaming polished wood, brass and luxury. 'Ze funnels. Do zey work?' enquires Inspector Hercule Tufnell. 'Oh yes,' says the skipper, 'well, not exactly ... as a matter of fact...' The ears of the ace left-arm-detective prick up.

'Pleeze be so good as to explain, mon capitaine.'

203

'Well, you see, Sir Paul is very keen on watching cricket on satellite television wherever and whenever he can…'

'Naturellement … Proceed.'

'Yes. In fact quite often he will make me trawl around the high seas until we get the best signal for the television reception…'

'Ah-ha. So. It eez as I suspected. Ze first funnel, she works perfectly well, non? But ze second funnel, zat is for housing ze satellite dish, n'est-ce pas?'

'Good lord, Monsieur Tufnell. How did you know?'

'Ze leetle grey cells, mon capitaine. Au revoir.'

In fact, not much left of ze leetle grey cells after far one or two glasses too many of the Bollinger. Still, rest day tomorrow. Au revoir, Sir Paul.

Thursday 19 March

There are many bad things about having to play back-to-back Test matches, namely that it's bloody hard work. But one good thing now is that we have no time to sulk about Barbados. What we must not do is go into the final Test in a negative frame of mind. If we do that, they WILL murder us.

A few of the lads go down to the ground in St John's to look at the relaid pitch. All the reports from the practice matches they organised here are okay, but we want to see for ourselves and the news is all good.

The pitch looks an absolute belter, a hard, true surface, just like Barbados, if not better, perfect conditions for us to repeat our performance there. Huge uplift to spirits and that is communicated in the team meeting.

We're keeping the same XI – after last week why wouldn't we? And what is impressed upon everyone is that we must go out there and get what we deserve.

Friday 20 March, Sixth Test, Recreation Ground, Day 1

Close of play: England 1st inns 35–2 (Stewart 18*, Headley 0*)

Atmosphere buzzing at the Recreation Ground, which has been substantially altered and improved since we were here last. Chikie's Disco gets going early and loud, although there is no sign yet of Gravy, the transvestite car mechanic who devises a new, ingenious and occasionally risqué ensemble in which to keep the crowd amused. Can't wait to see what gear he will be turning up in. Perhaps the outfit best recalled by England fans was one of his least exotic. Eight years ago when Robin Smith walked out for his second innings simple and England struggling against a fierce bombardment of pace bowling, he was surprised to find that he had not made the journey alone. Looking around he saw Gravy, dressed in whites and short-sleeve sweater, sporting a red motor-cycle crash-helmet and carrying a three-foot-wide bat.

We notice a couple of new stands filled to bursting with England supporters and an outfield like a billiard table.

BUT, what has happened to the pitch? It is not just damp, but wet. How?

Apparently just after the boys left the ground, the groundsman gave it one final watering prior to leaving it open for the sun to dry it and a nice night under the covers. What happened was that almost immediately after he did so, the heavens opened. He then had to put the covers on top of the damp pitch to stop it getting even wetter. But then the rain continued for the rest of the day and overnight, so there has been no chance for the sun to dry it. In the morning he took the covers off to find that the surface had sweated underneath them all night. He tries to tell us that the moisture on the pitch is morning dew, but since the strips either side of it are bone dry this does not quite compute.

And of course, the prevailing conditions now make winning the toss absolutely vital. This pitch, we think, is probably too wet to start the Test match. It will do everything early on, then, bearing in mind what we saw yesterday, it will almost certainly flatten out and play beautifully. So the toss is huge. And we lose it.

A brief shower delays the start by ten minutes. And then, for few minutes, it is Sabina Park all over again.

The first ball, from Courtney to Ath is short, sails past his head and pushes a dent out of the pitch. The fifth ball climbs off a good length and smacks into Ath's left forearm, just above the wrist. Now Ath never likes to let bowlers know that a blow has caused him pain. Just like me, really. So when he chucks his bat away and wanders away from the crease grimacing and calling for the fizz, you know that hurt. On comes Morton and down comes the rain.

The downpour is short and sharp and will clearly mean the outfield is too wet to resume for a while. But at least the emergence of the hot sun will enable the covers to be removed and the pitch to dry out some. For no reason we can fathom, however, they are kept on, which only means that the pitch will sweat some more, particularly in this humidity.

And it does. On the resumption, Courtney finishes his over. Then it's Amby's turn and more of the same. His third delivery takes another lump out of the surface, this one the size of a soup bowl. A couple of balls later, Al flings an arm up to fend one away from his head and punches it over the keeper for four. Once again our openers are being tested on pure courage rather than batsmanship. Both of them get hit time and again, the worst incident involving Al.

In the tenth over, shortly before the mercy of the lunch break, Amby makes one rear up straight past Al's bat and thud into an area just above his heart. By all the laws of physics it is a completely unplayable delivery. Al drops to his knees and for a few sickening moments, stays there, his head wedged against the ground by the weight of his body.

Morton races out without being asked and when he gets to Al he is clearly anxious. A few minutes pass before he is eventually helped to his feet and declares himself okay to continue. But inside the dressing room the reaction to that ball is chillingly reminiscent of the atmosphere at Sabina Park.

How we get to lunch without losing a wicket I will never know. What the hell is going to happen afterwards?

We have to wait some time to find out, as another half hour or so of rain during the interval leads, quite incredibly, to the entire post-lunch session being wiped out.

Very bizarre goings-on. First the mechanical 'water-hog' that had been working before lunch, suddenly stops. This leaves the mopping up of the water from the covers in the hands, literally, of the team of 'ground assistants' who turn out to be a dozen prisoners from the local jail.

Under the supervision of Antigua Cricket Board officials, they are given an assortment of household items such as sponges, buckets and what look suspiciously like flannels made from shammy leather. Perfect for those tricky smears on the window, I'm sure, but hardly the ideal equipment for trying to restart an international cricket match. With these they are supposed to clear all the surface water from the outfield and covers. It's like taking a mop to the Atlantic.

The crowning glory of all their efforts comes when the rain gang attempt to remove the covers. They all march to the outside of the square, grab hold of the sheets, pick them up and pull. And as they do so gallons of water that have gathered on top of the sheets gush forward and down all over the now unprotected square.

Don't get me wrong. I'm all for giving these 'victims of society' another crack of the whip. But it has become blindingly obvious by now that these blokes do not have the first idea what they are doing. The lake spreads quickly, and at one stage there is a real danger that it will cover the entire playing surface. In fact it comes to within only a few yards of the pitch before subsiding and seeping back into the soil.

Several bags of sawdust are duly sent for, then spread over the offending wet patches. Then another shower comes and the covers are put back on again. And off again shortly afterwards. They finally manage to boot some life back into the mechanical 'water hog' at about 3pm, but for one reason or another, mainly the fact that the sawdust-filled swamps need the time to dry out, we do not actually restart the match until 4.45, twenty minutes before the scheduled close of play. For any further information on the above, please contact the Frederick Karno Pitchcare co.

A very tricky little period to survive now, but if we can manage it we can start again tomorrow with minimal damage and hope intact. By then, if it is fine in the morning as forecast, the pitch might have dried out enough for a fairer contest.

Ath, who had batted brilliantly in the early skirmishes, escapes when miscuing one over the keeper. But from the first ball of the next over, from Amby, he is caught in the gully by Ramnarine. Three balls later, Butch, who has gone out and looked to dominate, slashes at one too close to him for the shot and is out for a duck.

We reach the close on 35 for two which is nothing like as bad as it might have been. In fact had we spent more time batting on that wet pitch we could well have been in real trouble. So when we return to the hotel, the feeling is that we are still in the game.

Saturday 21 March, Sixth Test, Day 2

England 1st inns 127 all out; West Indies 1st inns 126–0 (Wallace 67*, Lambert 46*)

Not a great day for us. The pitch does dry out, but only enough to allow the ball to grip and jag both ways. Curtly bowls fast leg-breaks more or less, and God knows how you are supposed to play them. But what is poor from our perspective and what must upset Athers is that we lose most of our main wickets to the leg-spin of Ramnarine.

Deano, in as nightwatchman, doesn't last too long and once Alec goes to Franklyn Rose in the over before lunch, the stuff we serve up afterwards is pretty dire.

I know from experience that spinners occasionally take wickets that, by right, belong to seamers. On a dodgy pitch batsmen are sometimes so relieved when the quicks are out of the equation that they chance their arm against us when otherwise they wouldn't. Maybe that is what we see here. To win the game we have to make runs, for sure, but perhaps our boys fell into the trap of chasing the game too early. Chalks has to be unlucky with his leg before to Ramnarine and his reaction to the decision earns him six-of-the-best from Jarman. Nass is brilliantly caught by Roland Holder, bit unlucky. But Ramps is so intent on attacking anything he can that he slaps a long-hop into the hands of cover of Walsh. The rest is mere subsidence and we are all out for 127, which is the lowest Test score ever recorded here and, on a pitch that is now drying fast, horribly insufficient. We've been rolled.

And then, Philo and Clayton go completely bananas.

Facing such a low total, they were always going to play positively. And, learning from events in Barbados we set the fielders a tad deeper for them. We may as well have put them on the moon. Carried on the sounds created by the All Saints Iron Band, banging away at anything they could find, and inspired in turn by the thumping of Chickie's Discomania and the lilting lyrical chanting of whatever Posse was now in town, Wallace and Lambert go wild.

Fraser's first ball is smashed through extra-cover for four, Lambert then launches Caddy over mid-wicket and it is all happening. The fifty comes up in the eighth over – excellent progress for a one-day international let alone a Test match. One or two of us might have been guilty of underestimating Philo. When we first came up against him I do believe the word 'slogger' might have been on one or two lips. Trouble is, lads, he keeps employing the middle of the bat.

By now there is nothing in the pitch and our seamers will be the first to admit they did not bowl especially well, but this is amazing stuff. Pre-meditated, hot-blooded assault. And the crowd is being whipped up into a complete frenzy.

I remember one shot in particular from Lambert because I really do believe it could have killed me. Early on, before they really got going, I am keenly fielding close to the action at mid-off to try and stop the short single off Caddy, when, out of the blue, Clayton absolutely mooses one straight at my head. Just in time, I manage to get a reasonable mit on the thing and, thinking I must have taken most of the pace off the ball, I turn and prepare to give chase. I've gone about a pace and a half when I see the ball clumping into the boundary board some forty yards away and then bouncing back about another thirty yards. At that point I suddenly realise that if the ball had hit me full-on there is a big chance this diary would have been published posthumously.

By the close of play, after twenty seven overs of this, they are 126 for nought, one run behind with ten wickets in the shed.

Sunday 22 March, Sixth Test, Day 3

West Indies 1st inns 451–5 (Hooper 85*, Holder 45)

An even worse day. Wallace, Lambert, Lara and Hoops all climb into us. The pitch is flat as a fart. We, me included, drop catches and look shoddy.

Respect to Philo, who goes for 92 when he deserved a hundred. Respect to Lambert, who takes full advantage of being dropped three times to make the century that is surely some compensation for the six-and-a-half years he has spent out of favour with their selectors. At 36, he's been given a second chance he can never have expected and he has taken it. Respect to Lara who bats like, well he bats like Lara, until Al pulls off a stunning catch at mid-wicket. Respect to Gravy who spends the afternoon dressed in a short skirt and white fishnet hold-up stockings, replaying every shot. Respect to Hoops, who has made a decision that he is going to enjoy himself, wallops Fraze back over his head almost as soon as he has taken guard and then just hits it everywhere.

But we are not at the races today. We're trying really hard, but with every minute and every mistake the feeling that it is all slipping away from us grows and grows. When that happens there is no hiding place and, every error, dropped catch, squandered run out chance, every bad ball, every big shot against you is magnified. No-one throws in the towel. We are all out there busting a gut, but when you get throttled for 127 and all of a sudden they are smacking it everywhere on a flat one with small boundaries, sometimes the edge just goes. In some ways playing for pride is worse than not turning up at all. This is hurting.

By the time Holder drills a return catch back to Caddy from the final ball of the day, they have made 451 for five, a not inconsiderable lead of 324, with five wickets left and two days to go. Odds on an England win? Don't answer that.

Monday 23 March, Sixth Test, Day 4

West Indies 1st inns 500–7 dec. (Hooper 108*, Ambrose 19*); England 2nd inns 173–3 (Hussain 54*, Thorpe 18*)
Today is Athers' 30th birthday. He's in pretty jovial mood considering. There is a look of resignation about him, though. Perhaps too many birthdays have come and gone with his side in the cart.

What's to say? Hoops carries on to reach his hundred. I bowl more containing stuff. Curtly takes them to 500 and the declaration by clubbing Fraze high into the Richie Richardson stand for six and we are left needing 373 to avoid an innings defeat. They have more than five sessions in which to bowl us out.

Now, the romantics among us have the following scenario in mind: Athers, under increasing pressure over the captaincy and his lack of form, walks out to bat with his dodgy back to the wall and a Test match to save. At close of play on the final day he is 185 not out, miraculously exactly the same score as he made at The Wanderers Ground, Johannesburg in December 1995, on the occasion of his greatest innings and one of the most memorable rearguard actions in the history of Test cricket.

And by lunch the image is still intact.

But then, Ath's nemesis on this trip, King Curt – come to think of it, whose nemesis isn't he? – pops the balloon.

Lara tries something different. We are 45 for none and coping and it is all a bit too comfortable for his liking. So he pulls the kind of stroke that gives captains a good name. He does something seemingly just for the sake of it and it comes off. Amby has bowled the entire match from the Northern

End, which is the end the Antiguan himself likes to bowl from. So Lara switches him to the Southern End. And with the first ball of his new spell, he traps Ath on the back foot. For thirteen. Happy Birthday, mate.

This is the sixth time Ath has fallen to Amby in eleven innings. Going in first on largely substandard pitches, he has made a total of 199 at an average of 18.09, somewhat different from last time here when he made 510 at 56.66, and as he trudges off, it shows. Just feel so sorry for the bloke. No-one could have tried harder. I think sometimes we forget that, when you strip everything else away, whoever is the captain of the England cricket team is just an ordinary broke as vulnerable and complicated and weak and strong as anyone else. On the television, even Beefy, who is a good mate of the captain, tells the viewers: 'He looks very tired and as though he is not enjoying it. Mike has done a tremendous job. But, personally I would get out at the end of this Test.' And for the first time, hearing those words has actually brought home to me that this is a real possibility. Only two Tests ago, after we had won in Trinidad to square the series, he was arriving in Georgetown, Guyana preparing to lead England for the fiftieth time. And now some of the same blokes who praised his stubbornness, stickability and determination are writing that the time has come for him to stand down. It's showbiz, I suppose, but talk about highs and lows...

Publicly at least, Graveney has insisted that no decision will be made until we get home. The way Ath looks now you get the feeling he might not want to wait that long.

Amby then gets rid of Butch for a King Curt-pair and we are 49 for two and a long way from home. This is Amby's thirtieth wicket of the series. Not bad for a bloke written off by home and English media before the start.

But these are not the conditions for another collapse. Not yet, anyway. The pitch has flattened out and as things settle down again, with Al playing some brilliant shots and Nass taking his time hopes rise again that we can save the match and save face. Al makes 79 before falling to Hoops, but Chalks and Nass bat really well from then to the close at which point we are 173 for 3 and still alive. Chalky's back is troubling him a considerable amount now and I wouldn't be at all surprised if he has to pull out of the one-day squads. To be fair I think he could probably do with the break anyway. He's played non-stop since we left for Zimbabwe two Novembers ago, including the Sharjah tournament, and he must be knackered.

Bumble is interviewed by the press boys and tells them: 'We owe it to ourselves to fight to the last and if we can get out of this match with a draw we will go home with our heads held high.'

And if we can't ?

So much is at stake. To be totally honest, if they have a full day at us and bowl well on a pitch that is now starting to offer, I will be very surprised if we can hang on. But you never know.

Tuesday 24 March, Sixth Test, Day 5

England 2nd inns 321 all out (Thorpe 84*). West Indies win by an innings and 52 runs. West Indies 3, England 1.
And a welcome sight greets us when we arrive at the ground. Rain. Lovely rain. The weather gods owe us one. Can you hear me? After Barbados, after the bog-up over watering the pitch here, you bloody owe us.

We do not start until after lunch, but because of the fact that when we are the side batting to avoid defeat the local regulations state that play can continue until the moon comes up, unfortunately for us, that only means losing one hour. Now, now, Philip.

Will the hour prove crucial?

At first, as the partnership between Nass and Chalks develops, it looks as though such thoughts constitute pessimism bordering on treachery. No-one, but no-one, is underestimating the ability of Curtly and Courtney to rewrite the plot in seconds, but between lunch and tea the boys bat with confidence and command and play some nifty shots too, cuts, pulls and hooks mixed in with the full-face block. Very nice. Twenty minutes before tea Nass collects his hundred, a really top knock, and twenty minutes afterwards they are still together. And then come the series of events that once again prove that, against these guys you are never safe until the groundsman has locked up his shed and gone home.

A bloody run out. Can you believe it? They've put on 167 and, including the weather, lasted six and a quarter hours together. Then a sodding run out renders all their efforts irrelevant. Chalks pushes the ball towards midwicket, Nass isn't sure and stop-starts all the way down. In the moment Hoops flicks back his underarm return to the keeper, Junior Murray, Nass and Chalks are in mid-pitch together. Nass makes a token effort to get there but no third umpire is necessary. 295 for four.

No panic yet, though. Ramps to come, then Jack, Deano and Caddy, not to mention Fraze, before me. Still only four down and less than a full session to survive no matter how many candles they light up on the terraces.

At this stage we are happy enough. But next over Ramps is done by Ramnarine and bowled for nought. 300 for five.

Not again. Not again, please.

And now enters Courtney, age 93, at the end of a long and draining series coming soon after a long and draining tour of

Pakistan, to bowl a yard or two quicker than at any other time all winter, possibly his quickest spell for years. The sight of the little chink of light appearing in the wall has just inspired him. Jack helps Chalks hang around, but Walsh is after his mate and he gets him next, leg before. 312 for six.

Lara now makes another of those moves that, at first sight, appear pointless, but turn out to be inspired. He switches Walsh to the other end. Why? Mind games, possibly, or maybe this: Walsh is now Lara's main chance. Amby looks spent. There will only be one chance to win this Test match and it is now. How to get the most out of the old boy? Get him kicking off from the end where Chickie's Disco is thumping and pumping. Any wickets now from him and they will raise the roof. And raise Walsh. What happened next? as they say. Has this bloke Lara got the magic touch, or what?

In the dressing room everything is happening so slowly. The balls, the overs just aren't moving. Deano goes in now, but already Caddy, Fraze and me are looking at each other and thinking exactly the same thoughts that we have thought too many times before. Then Deano gets out to Ramnarine, 313 for seven. Big noise from Chickie's disco. Here we go. Here we go. Here we go.

Then, a blur.

Caddy, caught behind, 316 for eight. More noise. Fraze, somehow, deflects one to the long-leg boundary for four. Then gets one in the snot-box. Then is caught by Chanderpaul. 320 for nine. More noise.

Here I go. The noise is absolutely deafening. Eight overs to survive. Come on, I can do this. In fact at this stage, strangely, I feel remarkably confident. Almost chipper. Pass Fraze on the way back who grunts.

Meet Chalks half way down the pitch to receive instructions.

'All right, mate?', I say.

'Yeah, I'm all right.' he says. ' Let's just play it as it comes'.

'Righto, mate.'

And then the complete lunacy of what he has just said hits me like a very fast bumper. 'Play it as it comes? What on earth is he talking about?'

I am out from the first delivery of the next over. Not totally sure I hit the ball, as it happens, but huge appeal, and by the time I look up to see if Bucknor is going to give me out, Courtney is running around with his arms stretched wide like a demented turkey. I look down to see that all the stumps have been removed then I look up again to see everyone charging off the field.

Walsh has finished with four for 80, and one wicket short of Malcolm Marshall's West Indies record of 376 Test victims and he's got the last three for spit to win them a game we thought we had saved by an innings and 52 runs. We have lost the series 3–1. Exactly the same as four years ago. Extremely disappointing. We all knew we should have drawn the game and we looked good enough to do it. And we have been absolutely blown away, losing our last six wickets for 26 runs in 3.7 nanoseconds.

When I get back to the dressing room I am just numb. A feeling of total despondency hangs everywhere. Then almost before I can pause to draw breath more sadness, this time overwhelming.

While we are milling about for the presentation ceremony, Ath spreads the word that he wants to have a chat with us in the dressing room straight afterwards.

Awards completed, we all duly assemble inside and wait for Ath. A hush comes down and Athers says to us: 'I'd just like to thank you all for your support on this tour. And I'd like to thank you for your support over the last four years.

I've decided to stand down as captain.'

Then, without uttering another word, he walks off to face the press and make his decision public, leaving the dressing-room in absolute, stunned silence.

After a few moments the shock turns to tears. Gus, Nass, even me. It was like a funeral in there.

Slowly you take in what Ath has said. Is it making any sense? Not really. Not yet. Then it does, in bits, in waves almost and gradually the feeling comes over everyone that we are in some way responsible, that somehow we have let him down.

Emotions are jumping. Everything is still unclear. What did he say? Thank us for our support? What?

Then, again, gutting sadness and quiet.

Until something like this happens, I don't think you realise just how close you get to people in this line of work. You are away from home together for months on end, sharing your aggravations as well as your successes, living in each other's pockets, sharing your innermost thoughts. You get *involved*. Ath is our captain (or was), but he is also our mate. Whether he is right or wrong to make the decision doesn't matter. Everything is a mess inside.

Looking at the television screen, I notice Ath arriving in the room where the press conference is being held. It's obvious he is struggling, he's swallowing hard. Finally, he gets the words out: 'After much consideration and after discussions with the chairman of selectors, David Graveney, I have decided to step down as captain with immediate effect. It's time for someone else to lead the side. A combination of our failure to win this series and my own form, which has been well below my previous standards, have led me to believe it is time for someone else to do the job.' Still can't take in the content of what he is saying but it just strikes me how tough it must be for him to go in there and offer himself up like this.

No sign of Bumble at this stage. He is very cut up, I hear. But chooses to air his grief in private. Only a game, my arse.

Start to try and make some sense out of what has happened. People said afterwards that Ath must have been relieved to have his life back and I think that is partly true. Only he knows how much the last four years have taken out of him, and, I suspect he is not the same bloke as he was back then and he is certainly not the bloke I went on my first senior tour with back in 1990–91. But, from a cricketing and personal point of view what really must hurt is coming to the conclusion that it is in the best interests of the side for you to give up the job. He has tried so hard to get things right and by standing down, he is obviously conceding that it hasn't worked out the way he wanted it to. Hard to take.

Every tour Ath has gone on as captain, every Test series he has started he must have believed that this was the one where things were going to come right. For him to have agreed to carry on at the end of last summer he must have believed that we were capable of winning here and no matter what the circumstances and how much has gone against us, the end result is that we have failed.

How many times can you pick yourself up again? When the rain came in Barbados did he feel he was just fated not to succeed, that this was not meant to happen for him? Perhaps this is just one fall too many.

Ath returns from the press conference and is bombarded by hugs and handshakes. No-one quite knows where to look, what to do, or what to say. Beers are passed round, some of their boys come in and have a chat and that takes a few minds off the bereavement, momentarily. Apart from a couple of moments, the spirit between the sides has been excellent, perhaps the best and most competitive I've played in. And the atmosphere between the players off the field has been brilliant. That says a lot for the relationship between Ath and Lara which has been very good – strong and tough on both sides when necessary, but overall solid. Their players are busting with the win but try not to show it too much which is good of them. Amby asks if he can swap a shirt with Gus which makes the big man feel a million bucks.

Later, when we are packing up to leave, someone makes a feeble joke to Athers about how he can now come out with the boys a bit more. Think it might have been me.

Sod it. Time to get lashed.

Thursday 26 March. Antigua to London Gatwick.

And so another tour draws to a close. For those not staying for the one-day matches, me included, it is a flight back to Barbados to pick up the gear we left at Rockley last week, then home on the early evening flight, which passes uneventfully and moderately soberly. With my reputation?

A few thoughts on the plane home ... How did I bowl? Did it come out alright? Bowled to contain mainly, but I would have been happier with a few more wickets. What could I have done differently? What should I have done differently? Was I agressive enough?

Was 3–1 fair? Cannot believe it was. Missed catches stick in your mind, decisions that went against us, bad luck with the tosses. But basically, at the end of it all you think to yourself, to hell with it.

Early morning arrival at Gatwick. And now the fantasy existence of touring with England is once again at an end. I receive my reality implants from officials at the airport then head for home.

Two hours later, for the first time in 80-odd days, I walk

220

in through my own front door.

I put down my bag, call out: 'Lisa, I'm back', then lean down to kiss Poppy.

She looks up at me, smiles and says: 'Bye, bye.'

Glossary of names

Ath, Athers – Mike Atherton
Nass – Nasser Hussain
Butch – Mark Butcher
Caddy – Andrew Caddick
Ash – Ashley Cowan
Creeps – John Crawley
Crofty – Robert Croft
Gus, Gusto, Fraze – Angus Fraser
Deano, Headless – Dean Headley
Smokes, Smokey – Adam Hollioake
Ramps – Mark Ramprakash
Jack – Jack Russell
Silvers – Chris Silverwood
Al, Stewie – Alec Stewart
Thorpey, Chalks – Graham Thorpe
The cat – me
Bumble – David Lloyd, coach
Embers, Ernie – John Emburey, assistant coach
Fizz – Wayne Morton, physio
Riddler – Dean Riddle, fitness co-ordinator
Beefy, Beef – Ian Botham
Murgers – Brian Murgatroyd, press officer
B.C. – Brian Lara
Amby, King Curt – Curtley Ambrose
Hoops – Carl Hooper